Gospel
Fictions

Gospel Fictions

RANDEL HELMS

 Prometheus Books

59 John Glenn Drive
Amherst, New York 14228-2197

Published 1988 by Prometheus Books

99 98 97 96   5 4 3 2

Library of Congress Cataloging-in-Publication Data

Helms, Randel, 1942–
    Gospel fictions / Randel Helms.
        p. cm.
    Bibliography: p.
    ISBN (invalid) 0–08975–464–8 (alk. paper)
    1. Bible. N.T. Gospels—Criticism, interpretations, etc. I. Title.
BS2555.2.2H38   1988
266′.066—dc19   88–19040
                                                                    CIP

Printed in the United States of America on acid-free paper

To Susan McCraw Helms

CONTENTS

CONTENTS

I

THE ART OF THE GOSPELS
Theology as Fictional Narrative

In the first century of the Common Era, there appeared at the eastern end of the Mediterranean a remarkable religious leader who taught the worship of one true God and declared that religion meant not the sacrifice of beasts but the practice of charity and piety and the shunning of hatred and enmity. He was said to have worked miracles of goodness, casting out demons, healing the sick, raising the dead. His exemplary life led some of his followers to claim he was a son of God, though he called himself the son of a man. Accused of sedition against Rome, he was arrested. After his death, his disciples claimed he had risen from the dead, appeared to them alive, and then ascended to heaven. Who was this teacher and wonder-worker? His name was Apollonius of Tyana; he died about 98 A.D., and his story may be read in Flavius Philostratus's *Life of Apollonius*.[1]

Readers who too hastily assumed that the preceding described
Apollonius's slightly earlier contemporary, Jesus of Nazareth, may
be forgiven their error if they will reflect how readily the human
imagination embroiders the careers of notable figures of the past
with common mythical and fictional embellishments. The career
of any remarkable person is remembered in oral tradition precisely
by being mythicised, connected with certain almost universally
known patterns. Mircea Eliade gives us the example of Dieudonne
de Gozon, a medieval Grand Master of the Knights of St. John
at Rhodes who, according to legend, slew the dragon of Malpasso.
It makes no difference, writes Eliade, that the genuine historical
record concerning Dieudonne is innocent of dragons; the mere
fact that the man was, in the popular imagination, a hero, necessarily
identified him with "a category, an archetype, which, entirely dis-
regarding his real exploits, equipped him with a mythical biography
from which it was *impossible* to omit combat with a reptilian
monster."[2]

We may say much the same of Jesus of Nazareth, though
without needing to insist that all the mythical biographies of this
figure *entirely* disregard his genuine acts. Moreover, I shall use
the word "fiction" rather than the word "myth" to refer to the
study, contained in this book, of the fictional aspects of the four
canonical Gospels. By fiction I mean—to put the matter in simplest
terms at the outset—a narrative whose purpose is less to describe
the past than to affect the present. Of course, all works of fiction
have an element of history, all works of history an element of
fiction.[3] The Gospels, however—and this is my thesis—are largely
fictional accounts concerning an historical figure, Jesus of Nazareth,
intended to create a life-enhancing understanding of his nature.
The best biblical statement of the purpose of a gospel is found
in the Gospel of John:

There were indeed many other signs that Jesus performed in the presence
of his disciples, which are not recorded in this book. Those here written

have been recorded in order that you may hold the faith that Jesus
is the Christ, the Son of God, and that through this faith you may
possess life by his name (John 20:30–31 NEB)

This is a noble intention, and it is not my purpose here to articulate
a quarrel with Christian faith, or to call the evangelists liars, or
to assert that the Gospels have *no* historical content; I write as
literary critic, not as debunker. The Gospels are, it must be said
with gratitude, works of art, the supreme fictions in our culture,
narratives produced by enormously influential literary artists who
put their art in the service of a theological vision. It is, of course,
not uncommon to recognize literary artistry in the Gospels; there
is perhaps no more beautiful short story than "The Prodigal Son,"
no more moving sentence in all world literature than "I am with
you always, until the end of time" (Matt. 28:20). But what does
it *mean* to say that the evangelists were literary artists? Literary
artists use their imaginations to produce poetry and fiction, works
open to the methods of literary criticism. The Gospels are, indeed—
and to a much greater degree than those who read them with
pious inattention even begin to realize—imaginative literature, fiction, and critics have been using such terms about them for a
long time. B. H. Streeter, for example, wrote more than half a
century ago about the role of the "creative imagination" in the
composition of the Fourth Gospel.[4] Reginald Fuller has, more
recently, examined the extent to which the Resurrection narratives
are the "free creation" of the evangelists.[5] Norman Perrin has
declared that his approach to the Gospels, Redaction Criticism,
looks for the "composition of new material" by the evangelists.[6]
I write in a similar spirit.

Each of the four canonical Gospels is religious proclamation
in the form of a largely fictional narrative. Christians have never
been reluctant to write fiction about Jesus, and we must remember
that our four canonical Gospels are only the cream of a large
and varied literature. We still possess, in whole or in part, such

works as the Gospel of Thomas, the Gospel of Peter, the Gospel of Philip, the Secret Gospel of Mark, the Gospel of Mary Magdalene, and such anonymous gospels as those according to the Hebrews, the Egyptians, the Ebionites, and so on. Jesus is the subject of a large—in fact, still growing—body of literature, often unorthodox or pure fantasy, cast in the form of fictional narrative and discourse.

This literature was oral before it was written and began with the memories of those who knew Jesus personally. Their memories and teachings were passed on as oral tradition for some forty years or so before achieving written form for the first time in a self-conscious literary work, so far as we know, in the Gospel of Mark, within a few years of 70 A.D.[7]

But oral tradition is by definition unstable, notoriously open to mythical, legendary, and fictional embellishment. We know that by the forties of the first century traditions already existed which we would now label orthodox and traditions coming to be recognized as heretical—teachings about what Jesus said and meant that even then were being called (though in a different vocabulary) "fictional." Paul, for example, writing to the Galatians about 50 A.D., declares, "I am astonished to find you turning so quickly away from him who called you by grace, and following a different gospel" (Galatians 1:6). Thirty or forty years later, Luke too was aware of both valid and invalid traditions about Jesus, aware that some kinds of information about Jesus were more accurate than others:

> Many writers have undertaken to draw up an account of the events that have happened among us, following the traditions handed down to us by the original eyewitnesses and servants of the Gospel. And so I in my turn, your Excellency, as one who has gone over the whole course of these events in detail, have decided to write a connected narrative for you, so as to give you authentic knowledge about the matters of which you have been informed (Luke 1:1–4).

Luke apparently knew about information not "authentic" and narratives not "connected"; if the works of those "many writers" had indeed been satisfactory, Luke's account would be superfluous. Luke was obviously writing during a time when literature about Jesus was flowering, and some of it was unacceptable to him.

Luke is the only evangelist who tells us explicitly his methods of composition: He went to his sources, including at least some of those "many writers," closely examining them for accuracy, for the purpose of writing a "connected" narrative, one that is well organized either logically or chronologically (*kathexēs* could mean either). Luke might seem to be claiming eyewitness testimony as the basis for his Gospel, but in fact he is not; he only claims to possess traditions which he identifies as being handed down from the time of eyewitnesses—and for Luke, one of the eyewitnesses was Paul, who never saw the man whom moderns call the "historical Jesus."

Paul was an ecstatic visionary who experienced, for what seems to be a period of nearly thirty years after the death of Jesus, visions of a heavenly being he called "Christ" and "the Lord," and the fact is that neither Paul nor any other first-century Christian felt a need to distinguish between the heavenly being and the "historical Jesus." Paul gives the following account of one of his ecstatic experiences:

> I shall go on to tell of visions and revelations granted by the Lord. I know a Christian man who fourteen years ago (whether in the body or out of it, I do not know—God knows) was . . . caught up into paradise, and heard words so secret, that human lips may not repeat them.

He then admits it was he who had this experience and reveals the words of Jesus in one such vision: "My grace is all you need" (2 Cor. 12:1–4, 9). This is "eyewitness" testimony of a saying of Jesus, one obviously not recorded in the Gospels. What follows is another first-century "eyewitness" account of Jesus:

> Then I saw standing in the very middle of the throne, inside the circle
> of living creatures and the circle of elders, a Lamb with the marks
> of slaughter upon him. He had seven horns and seven eyes. (Rev. 5:6)

We can do no better than to bring our literary judgment to bear
on such accounts, using the concept of two different kinds of
figures—the historical Jesus and the visionary Christ—in a way
the first century did not. When we return to Luke's first chapter,
we should perhaps recognize anew that there are both the "historical
Jesus" and the Jesus of Luke's traditions, who has the same status
as the figures known to Paul and John the apocalypt. I will obviously
need to justify such a statement, and again the best way to begin
is with Paul's notion of the three ways of knowing about Jesus:
personal revelation, tradition, and the scriptures:

> I must make it clear to you, my friends [he writes to the Galatians],
> that the gospel you heard me preach is no human invention. I did
> not take it over from any man; no man taught it to me; I received
> it through a revelation of Jesus Christ. (Gal. 1:11-12)

The major contents of that gospel he lists in another letter:

> I must remind you of the gospel that I preached to you; the gospel
> which you received. . . .
>   First and foremost, I handed on to you the facts which had been
> imparted to me: That Christ died for our sins, in accordance with the
> scriptures; and that he was buried; that he was raised to life on the
> third day, according to the scriptures; and that he appeared to Cephas,
> and afterwards to the Twelve. (I Cor. 15:1-5)

And what was the source of the "facts which had been imparted"
to Paul? Four chapters earlier in I Corinthians, he had written
that "the tradition which I handed on to you came to me from
the Lord himself" (I Cor. 11:23).

So we must understand that what Luke means by "eyewitnesses," and what he means by doing historical research, comparing sources, and judging the accuracy of those sources, is not the same as what a modern historian would mean by the same terms. What one learns from the "traditions handed down to us from the original eyewitnesses" must be seen as having the same status, for a first-century thinker like Luke or Paul, as information gained from visions and from reading the scriptures for predictions of Jesus. The Gospels are about the figure composed from these three strands of information; they are not about the "historical Jesus." And that figure is a complex series of fictional creations; in the case of the canonical Gospels, there are at least four figures called "Jesus."

An example will help explain.

The canonical Gospels exist as sequences of narrative and dramatic scenes. This is not surprising: how else would one tell the "story" of Jesus? What is surprising is the great differences among the stories, even though they share, for the most part, similar sources. For example, according to Matthew and Mark, the dying words of Jesus were, "My God, my God, why hast thou forsaken me?" According to Luke, Jesus' dying words were "Father, into your hands I commit my spirit." But according to John, they were, "It is accomplished." To put it another way, we cannot know what the dying words of Jesus were, or even whether he uttered any; it is not that we have too little information, but that we have too much. Each narrative implicitly argues that the others are fictional. In this case at least, it is inappropriate to ask of the Gospels what "actually" happened; they may pretend to be telling us, but the effort remains a pretense, a fiction.

The matter becomes even more complex when we add to it the virtual certainty that Luke knew perfectly well what Mark had written as the dying words, and the likelihood that John also knew what Mark and perhaps Luke wrote, but that both Luke and John chose to tell the story differently. As it happens, all the death scenes were constructed to show Jesus dying the model death and doing so "in fulfillment" of Scripture. What this means I shall discuss

later, but for now, suffice it that the scenes have a religious and
moral purpose disguised as a historical one; we are, with these
scenes, in the literary realm known as fiction, in which narratives
exist less to describe the past than to affect the present. In De
Quincy's phrase, the Gospels are not so much literature of knowledge as literature of power.

As in the case mentioned above, the content of the Gospels
is frequently not "Jesus" but "what certain persons in the first century
wanted us to think about Jesus." In the language of the Fourth
Gospel, "Those [narratives] here written have been recorded in
order that you may hold the faith that Jesus is the Christ, the
Son of God" (John 20:31). In the language of literary criticism,
the Gospels are self-reflexive; they are not about Jesus so much
as they are about their own attitudes concerning Jesus.

That reflexive aspect of the Gospels is one of the main themes
of this book. I deal with the effort of the evangelists to present
their works to us as self-conscious literary documents, deliberately
composed as the culmination of a literary and oral tradition, echoing
and recasting that tradition, both appealing to it and transcending
it, while using it in multiple ways. The Gospels are Hellenistic
religious narratives in the tradition of the Greek Septuagint version
of the Old Testament, which constituted the "Scriptures" to those
Greek-speaking Christians who wrote the four canonical Gospels
and who appealed to it, explicitly or implicitly, in nearly every
paragraph they wrote.

A simple example is the case of the last words of Christ. Mark
presents these words in self-consciously realistic fashion, shifting
from his usual Greek into the Aramaic of Jesus, transliterated into
Greek letters: *Elōi elōi lama sabachthanei* (My God, my God, why
hast thou forsaken me?—Mark 15:34). Mark gives us no hint that
Jesus is "quoting" Psalm 22:1; we are clearly to believe that we
are hearing the grieving outcry of a dying man. But the author
of Matthew, who used Mark as one of his major written sources,
is self-consciously "literary" in both this and yet another way: though

using Mark as his major source for the passion story, Matthew is fully aware that Mark's crucifixion narrative is based largely on the Twenty-second Psalm, fully aware, that is, that Mark's Gospel is part of a literary tradition (this description would not be Matthew's vocabulary, but his method is nonetheless literary). Aware of the tradition, Matthew concerned himself with another kind of "realism" or verisimilitude. When the bystanders heard Jesus crying, according to Mark, to "*Elōi*," they assumed that "he is calling Elijah [*Eleian*]" (Mark 15:35). But Matthew knew that no Aramaic speaker present at the Cross would mistake a cry to God (*Elōi*) for one to Elijah—the words are too dissimilar. So Matthew self-consciously evoked yet another literary tradition in the service both of verisimilitude and of greater faithfulness to the Scriptures: not the Aramaic of Psalm 22:1 but the Hebrew, which he too transliterated into Greek—*Ēli Ēli* (Matt. 27:46)—a cry which could more realistically be confused for "*Ēleian*." Matthew self-consciously appeals both to literary tradition—a "purer" text of the Psalms—and to verisimilitude as he reshapes Mark, his literary source. The author of Mark was apparently unaware that his account of the last words was edifying fiction (a "fulfillment" of Scripture—see my chapter 6), but Matthew certainly knew that he was creating a linguistic fiction in his case (Jesus spoke Aramaic, not Hebrew), though just as clearly he felt justified in doing so, given his conviction that since Psalm 22 had "predicted" events in the crucifixion, it could be appealed to even in the literary sense of one vocabulary rather than another, as a more "valid" description of the Passion.

Luke is even more self-consciously literary and fictive than Matthew in his crucifixion scene. Though, as I have said, he knew perfectly well what Mark had written as the dying words of Jesus, he created new ones more suitable to his understanding of what the death of Jesus meant—an act with at least two critical implications: First, that he has thus implicitly declared Mark's account a fiction; second, that he self-consciously presents his own as a fiction. For like Matthew, Luke in 23:46 deliberately placed his

own work in the literary tradition by quoting Psalm 30 (31):5 in
the Septuagint as the dying speech of Jesus: "Into your hands
I will commit my spirit" (*eis cheiras sou parathēsomai to pneuma
mou*), changing the verb from future to present (*paratithemai*) to
suit the circumstances and leaving the rest of the quotation exact.
This is self-conscious creation of literary fiction, creation of part
of a narrative scene for religious and moral rather than historical
purposes. Luke knew perfectly well, I would venture to assert,
that he was not describing what happened in the past; he was
instead creating an ideal model of Christian death, authorized both
by doctrine and by literary precedent.

The creation of narrative and dramatic scenes to express the
"real" or inner (theological) meaning of a situation—this is a pretty
fair definition of one kind of fiction-writing. There was of course
a particular intellectual framework, a justifying worldview, behind
such fictive creation in the Gospels, one that allowed the evangelists
and the oral and literary traditions behind them to create stories
with full confidence they were telling the "truth"; first-century
Christians believed that the career of Jesus, even down to minor
details, was predicted in their sacred writings. By a remarkably
creative fiat of interpetation, the Jewish scriptures (especially in
Greek translation) became a book that had never existed before,
the *Old* Testament, a book no longer about Israel but about Israel's
hope, the Messiah, Jesus. Of course, many had found in the Jewish
scriptures the hope and prediction of a Messiah, but never before
was it specifically Jesus of Nazareth. So the story of Jesus came
into being as a mirror of the Old Testament; the Gospels closed
the self-reflexive circle: Old Testament-New Testament. Outside
the Gospels, the best New Testament examples of this kind of
thinking appear in the letters of Paul, all of which predate the
writing of the canonical Gospels. Speaking, for example, of the
miraculous provision of manna and water in the wilderness during
the Exodus, Paul wrote that all the Israelites

ate the same supernatural food, and all drank the same supernatural drink; I mean, they all drank from the supernatural rock that accompanied their travels—and that rock was Christ. . . . All these things that happened to them were symbolic [*typikōs*—"types"], and were recorded for our benefit as a warning. For upon us the fulfillment of the ages has come. (I Cor. 30:3–4,11)

The Old Testament event or character is the "type"; the New Testament fulfillment, usually an event or symbol in the life of Jesus, or of the first-century Christian, the "antitype," a word which appears at I Peter 3:21, where the water of our baptism is the "*antitypon*" of the waters of the flood. "For," Paul wrote, "all the ancient scriptures were written for our own instruction" (Rom. 15:4). The Old Testament was not, that is, aimed at general future audiences in all the ages, but specifically at first-century Christians, with messages intended directly for them. For Paul, the story of Adam was not merely the history of past things; Adam was a "type [*typos*] of him who was to come"—Christ (Rom. 5:14). Northrop Frye nicely sums up this self-reflexive aspect of the two Testaments as early Christians saw them:

> How do we know that the Gospel story is true? Because it confirms the prophecies of the Old Testament. But how do we know that the Old Testament prophecies are true? Because they are confirmed by the Gospel story. Evidence, so called, is bounced back and forth between the testaments like a tennis ball; and no other evidence is given us. The two testaments form a double mirror, each reflecting the other but neither the world outside.[8]

Such a view of the Old Testament allowed it to supply the basis for entire scenes in the fictively historical books of the New. A voice, for example, in the (now) "Old" Testament became by interpretive fiat the voice of Jesus: when the psalmist wrote "My flesh shall rest in hope: because thou wilt not leave my soul in hell, neither wilt thou suffer thine holy one to see corruption"(Psalms

15 [16]:9–10 LXX), it was in fact not "really" the psalmist speaking, but Jesus, a thousand years before his birth. As Luke has Peter say, in interpreting these verses to the crowd at Pentecost:

> Let me tell you plainly, my friends, that the patriarch David died and was buried, and his tomb is here to this very day. It is clear therefore that he spoke as a prophet, . . . and when he said he was not abandoned to death, and his flesh never suffered corruption, he spoke with foreknowledge of the resurrection of the Messiah. (Acts 2:29–31)

By fiat of interpretation, a psalm becomes a prophecy, David becomes Jesus. We see a two-stage creative process here: first, the psalm is turned into a prophetic minidrama; then the interpretation of the psalm becomes another dramatic scene: Peter explaining it to the multitude. That the fictive creative act is Luke's, and not Peter's, is clear from the Greek of the scene: Luke has Peter quote, fairly loosely, as if from memory, the Septuagint Greek text of the Psalms (though the historical Peter spoke Aramaic and needed, Christian tradition tells us, a Greek interpreter); the point of Luke's interpretation depends on the Greek text of the verse, not on the Hebrew. The Hebrew text of Psalm 16:10b has something like "nor suffer thy faithful servant to see the pit," which stands in simple parallelism to the first line of the distich, "Thou wilt not abandon me to Sheol"—that is, you will not allow me to die. The Greek text could, however, be taken to mean "You will not let me remain in the grave, nor will you let me rot." Peter's speech is an effective work of dramatic fiction, the culmination of a complex two-stage creative process. Luke, as we shall see, creates the same kinds of dramatic fictions in his Gospel, the first half of the Christian history that includes his Acts of the Apostles.

Not only speeches, but entire dramatic scenes grew out of the early Christian imaginative understanding of the Old Testament. This is true of the famous story of Peter's vision in Acts, chapter ten. There, Peter is commissioned in a vision to bear God's message of salvation to Cornelius, the first Gentile convert in Acts. On the basis of his conviction that the Greek Septuagint Old Testament was really a book predictive of his own time, Luke, or his source, created a narrative by simply rewriting portions of the Septuagint and setting them in the first century. Aware, for example, of Cornelius as an important early Gentile convert and convinced that his conversion was part of the providence of God, early Christians could quite easily suppose that the events leading up to Cornelius's conversion were already described in the Old Testament—in this case, the Book of Ezekiel. As the prelude to his prophetic role, Ezekiel has a series of visions; in the first of them, he sees the heavens open (*ēnoichthēsan hoi ouranoi*—Ezek. 1:1 LXX). Peter, about to receive his prophetic commission to go to the Gentile Cornelius, also sees in a vision the "heaven opened" (*tēn ouranon aneōgmenon*—Acts 10:11). In his next vision Ezekiel is shown something and told to "eat" (*phage*—Ezek. 2:9 LXX); similarly, in Peter's vision he is shown something and told to "eat" (*phage*—Acts 10:13). Ezekiel is told to eat "unclean" food, bread baked with human dung, but the prophet strongly demurs, saying "By no means, Lord" (*Mēdamōs, Kyrie*—Ezek. 4:14 LXX), just as Peter is told in his vision to eat unclean food, but likewise refuses: "By no means, Lord" (*Mēdamōs, Kyrie*—Acts 10:14). Ezekiel explains that he has never touched any "uncleanness" (*akatharsia*—Ezek. 4:14 LXX), just as Peter declares he has never eaten anything "unclean" (*akatharton*—Acts 10:14). Ezekiel's vision and commission became, by fiat of interpretation and narrative invention, Peter's. The creative act began as a critical act: Ezekiel's vision had to be identified as "really" about Peter's; the narrative invention then followed readily. Invention of that kind is the subject of this book.

II

How to Begin a Gospel

A central working hypothesis of this book and one of the most widely held findings in modern New Testament study is that Mark was the first canonical Gospel to be composed and that the authors of Matthew and Luke (and possibly John) used Mark's Gospel as a written source. As B. H. Streeter has said of this view of Mark:

> Its full force can only be realized by one who will take the trouble to go carefully through the immense mass of details which Sir John Hawkins has collected, analyzed, and tabulated, pp. 114-153 of his classic *Horae Synopticae.* How anyone who has worked through those pages with a synopsis of the Greek text can retain the slightest doubt of the original and primitive character of Mark, I am unable to comprehend. . . . The facts seem only explicable on the theory that each author had before him the Marcan material already embodied in a single document.[1]

Such a view of Mark underlies most worthwhile modern critical study of the Gospels, making it possible for us to see clearly, for the first time in nineteen centuries, what Matthew, Luke, and (in a different way) John were about as writers and how as literary artists they used sources. To study how the evangelists wrote, we must begin with Mark.

When the author of Mark set about writing his Gospel, circa 70 A.D., he did not have to work in an intellectual or literary vacuum. The concept of mythical biography was basic to the thought-processes of his world, both Jewish and Graeco-Roman, with an outline and a vocabulary already universally accepted: a heavenly figure becomes incarnate as a man and the son of a deity, enters the world to perform saving acts, and then returns to heaven. In Greek, the *lingua franca* of the Mediterranean world, such a figure was called a "savior" (*sōtēr*), and the statement of his coming was called "gospel" or "good news" (*euangelion*). For example, a few years before the birth of Jesus of Nazareth, the Provincial Assembly of Asia Minor passed a resolution in honor of Caesar Augustus:

> Whereas the Providence which has guided our whole existence and which has shown such care and liberality, has brought our life to the peak of perfection in giving to us Augustus Caesar, whom it [Providence] filled with virtue [*arete*] for the welfare of mankind, and who, being sent to us and to our descendants as a savior [*sōtēr*], has put an end to war and has set all things in order; and whereas, having become visible [*phaneis,* i.e., now that a God has become visible] . . . ; and whereas, finally that the birthday of the God (viz., Caesar Augustus) has been for the whole world the beginning of the gospel [*euangelion*] concerning him, (therefore, let all reckon a new era beginning from the date of his birth).[2]

A few years earlier, Horace wrote an ode in honor of the same Caesar Augustus which presents him as an incarnation of the god Mercury and outlines the typical pattern of mythical biography:

Which of the Gods now shall the people summon
To prop Rome's reeling sovereignty? . . .
Whom shall Jupiter appoint
As instrument of our atonement? . . .
thou, (Mercury), winged boy of gentle Maia.
Put on the mortal shape of a young Roman;
Descend, and well contented to be known
As Caesar's avenger,
Stay gladly and long with Romulus's people,
Delay thy homeward, skybound journey.[3]

Descent as son of a god appointed by the chief deity to become incarnate as a man, atonement, restoration of a sovereignty, ascension to heaven—a gospel indeed, and so like the pattern of the Christian Gospels!

The standard phrase "the beginning of the gospel" (*archē tou euangeliou*) of Caesar (or whomever) seems to have been widespread in the Graeco-Roman world. A stone from the marketplace of Priene in Asia Minor reads: "The birthday of the god (Augustus) was for the world the beginning of *euangelion* because of him."[4] Mark uses the same formula to open his book: "The beginning of the gospel [*Archē tou euangeliou*] of Jesus Christ the Son of god [*theou hyios*]." Even the Greek phrase "son of god" was commonly used for Augustus; on a marble pedestal from Pergamum is carved: "The Emperor Caesar, son of God (*theou hyios*), god Augustus."[5] Mark begins his mythical biography of Jesus with ready-made language and concepts, intending perhaps a challenge: *euangelion* is not of Caesar but of Christ!

But of course there was as much a Jewish cultural background for the concept of the descending-ascending heavenly redeemer as there was a Graeco-Roman. Heavenly figures who appear as men, perform saving acts, and then return to heaven are equally common in Jewish mythology. In the first-century-B.C. Book of Tobit, the angel Raphael comes from God to appear as the man Azarias ("Yahweh helps"), curing Tobit's blindness and driving away a demon from his daughter-in-law Sarah:

"God sent me to cure both you and Sarah your daughter-in-law at the same time. I am Raphael, one of the seven angels who stand in attendance on the Lord. . . . I am ascending to him who sent me." (Tobit 13:14-15,20)

If the outline of such soteriological mythology is a culturally-conditioned fiction (incarnate descent, saving acts, return to heaven), what of the particular contents of mythical biography as we have them in the Gospel of Mark? Certainly, there lived a Jesus of Nazareth, who was baptized in the Jordan by John, who taught, in imitation of John, that "the kingdom of God is upon you" (Mark 1:15); and who was killed by the Romans as a potentially dangerous fomentor of revolution. Of the outline of Jesus' life itself, this is just about all that Mark knew. Mark possessed a good many fictional (and some non-fictional) stories about Jesus and a small stock of sayings attributed to him, and he incorporated them in his Gospel; but he had no idea of their chronological order beyond the reasonable surmise that the baptism came at the beginning of the ministry and the crucifixion at the end. Mark is, in other words, not a biography; its outline of Jesus' career is fictional and the sequence has thematic and theological significance only. As Norman Perrin bluntly puts it, "The outline of the Gospel of Mark has no historical value."[6] Anyone can demonstrate this with a careful reading of Mark, watching the transitional tags between episodes. The following selection of them are translations from the New English Bible:

- "When after some days" (2:1)
- "Once more" (2:13)
- "When" (2:15)
- "Once, when" (2:18)
- "One Sabbath" (2:23)
- "One another occasion" (3:1)
- "On another occasion" (4:1)
- "When he was alone" (4:10)

- "That [unspecified] day" (4:35)
- "He left that place" (6:1)
- "On one of his teaching journeys" (6:6)
- "On another occasion" (7:14)
- "There was another occasion about this time" (8:1)
- "Jesus and his disciples set out" (8:27)
- "On leaving those parts" (10:1)
- "As he was starting out on a journey" (10:17)

Only after the tenth chapter, when Jesus enters Jerusalem to be arrested and crucified, does Mark present a circumstantial, sometimes hourly, chronology, and it appears likely, as we shall see, that there were fictional and theological reasons for this too.

Though he had reasons other than chronology for the structure or outline of his Gospel, Mark certainly knew what to put first: "The beginning of the Gospel of Jesus Christ, the Son of God" (Mark 1:1). But Mark's beginning comes when Jesus is already a grown man only a few months away from death, his Gospel says nothing about Jesus' birth or childhood, has almost no meaningful chronology, presents very little of Jesus' moral teaching (no Sermon on the Mount, no parables of the Prodigal Son or Good Samaritan), and has a spectacularly disappointing ending: the Resurrection, announced only by a youth, is witnessed by no one, and the women who were told about it "said nothing to anybody, for they were afraid" (Mark 16:8). End of Gospel. It is not difficult to grasp what Streeter means by the "original and primitive" character of Mark as compared to the other Gospels. It is this aspect of Mark's Gospel that I will describe in the next few pages.

Mark wrote some forty years after the Crucifixion, when Jesus was already rapidly becoming a figure of legend. Accurate firsthand information was hard to come by. Moreover, we must make an imaginative leap to grasp some of the thought processes of the first century. Modern concepts of historical research did not exist, and the understanding of history apparent in the Gospels is not what we would recognize today as "history." As Luke writes in the episode on the road to Emmaus:

> "Was the Messiah not bound to suffer thus before entering upon his glory?" Then he began with Moses and all the prophets, and explained to them the passages which referred to himself in every part of the scriptures. (Luke 24:26-27)

Even if they had known how, early Christians would not have felt obliged to conduct the kind of historical research that might be done by a modern to find information about Jesus; they had a divinely certified source already in their possession—the Jewish Bible, which most of them after about 50 A.D. read in Greek—which the early Christians, by remarkably creative interpretation, turned into a new book that had never existed before, the *Old* Testament, a book about Jesus. Not only the Prophets, but any part of the Hebrew scriptures was subject to being reinterpreted for reference to Jesus. Luke has Peter declare that even the author of Psalm 16 "spoke as a prophet" (Acts 2:30) about Christ.

The early Christians *could* have found out what we would call historical information about Jesus, but in fact they did not. It is not that their methods were slipshod—they read the Old Testament very carefully; it is that their methods were not historical. They composed imaginative fiction using a method of getting at the past that involved the creative interpretation of ancient texts read as oracular. Even in those places where historical memory exists in the Gospels, it is structured not according to history but according to a theological pattern dictated by a specific understanding of the Old Testament or other ancient texts.

We can see this in the way Mark began his Gospel:

> In the prophet Isaiah it stands written: "Here is my herald whom I send on ahead of you, and he will prepare your way. A voice crying aloud in the wilderness, 'Prepare a way for the Lord; clear a straight path for him.'" (Mark 1:2-3)

Mark uncritically used an already-composed account of John the Baptist (whether written or oral is unclear), which was, in a remarkably free fashion, based on the Old Testament. Typically, Mark did not consult directly the text of Isaiah, for he is clearly unaware that half his quotation, supposedly from Isa. 40:3, is not from Isaiah at all, but is a misquotation of Malachi 3:1, which actually reads, "I am sending my messenger who will clear a path before me." Mark's source has used Malachi as the basis for an interpretation of John the Baptist, changed Malachi to suit his needs, and composed in the process a piece of theological fiction. The ascription to Malachi probably dropped out during oral transmission (or through scribal carelessness), and Mark uncritically repeated the error.

Why didn't Mark do his own research? The answer is, of course, that by his standards he did: he went to the sources available to him. It was known, or at least believed, that Jesus was baptized by John in the Jordan, as were hosts of others, in the third or fourth decade of the first century, and this was a troubling fact. Neither Mark nor anyone else in his Christian community (perhaps circa 70 A.D. Rome) had been in Palestine at the time; all the participants were now dead, and Mark had a book to write. Fortunately, Mark's community possessed—as, we may suppose, all early Christian groups did—a stock of traditions about Jesus speaking and acting; among them, apparently, a brief narrative or set of narratives about his baptism. Indeed, Mark may even have had at his disposal a variety of competing accounts of this episode. We know that this was so in other instances, as in his accounts of the feeding of the five thousand in chapter 6 and of the four thousand in chapter 8, two different versions of the same legend that Mark accepted as altogether different stories (see my chapter 4 below). Mark may also have had to choose from among a variety of accounts of the baptism. Here, for example, is the surviving portion of the baptism account in the Gospel according to the Hebrews:

When the Lord ascended from the water, the whole fount of the Holy
Spirit descended and rested upon him and said to him: "My son, in
all the prophets I was waiting for you, that you might come, and that
I might rest in you. For you are my rest; and you are my firstborn
son, who reigns forever."[7]

This gospel was probably written in the early second century and
survives only in fragmentary quotations in such early writers as
Clement and Origen, but it may well have been based on the same
kinds of traditions Mark used. Christians have never been reluctant
to write fiction about Jesus, and Mark drew from a rich supply
of episodes, some of them perhaps like this one.

Why did Mark choose what he did? Probably for theological
reasons: John the Baptist presented genuine problems. Since the
baptism made John look like the mentor of Jesus and the initiator
of his career, the Baptist had to be demoted, but not too much;
the initiator became the divinely-predicted forerunner. Mark's
method of performing that demotion is fascinating because, para-
doxically, it does in fact the opposite, and had to be corrected,
three different ways, by the other three evangelists.

The baptism itself was the first awkward fact. Ordinarily, John's
baptism stood as a sign that one had repented of sin: "A baptism
in token of repentance, for the forgiveness of sins" (Mark 1:4).
It appears not to have troubled Mark that he presented Jesus as
a repentant sinner: people "flocked" to John, "and were baptized
by him in the River Jordan, confessing their sins. . . . It happened
at this time that Jesus came from Nazareth in Galilee and was
baptized in the Jordan by John" (Mark 1:5, 9). We have three
choices in interpreting this: Either Mark did not realize what he
was saying (the least likely), or he had not developed a theology
of Jesus' sinlessness (also unlikely, since Paul, who seems to have
influenced Mark's thinking, had such a theology twenty years
earlier), or he believed that Jesus *became,* or was certified, only
at the baptism, a new and different being over whom sin had

no power—the Son of God. This last interpretation is strongly implied by what follows the baptism:

> At the moment when he came up out of the water, he saw the heavens torn open and the Spirit, like a dove, descending upon him. And a voice spoke from heaven: "Thou art my Son, my Beloved; on thee my favor rests." (Mark 1:10-11)

Obviously a major theme in Mark is Jesus' divine sonship; Jesus' earthly ministry is presented as beginning with this declaration at the baptism, and ending with the soldier's declaration at the Cross: "Truly this man was the Son of God" (Mark 15:39). When did Jesus become "Son of God"? The answer, for at least some early Christians, lies in the source of the heavenly speech, that impressive fiction about the divine voice and its declaration.

Since neither Mark nor anyone he knew was with Jesus at this time in his career, Mark had to resort to the traditions about Jesus, which had been composed as a string of imaginative enlargements on passages from the Old Testament and the Jewish apocrypha. It is apparent that at least some of the early Christians regarded Jesus' baptism as the ritual whereby he was appointed Son of God and King of Israel. Early Christians seem to have accepted the traditional Jewish notion that Yahweh's messiah (Israel's king) was called the Son of God. The notion is presented in its clearest form in Yahweh's prophecy to Nathan about Solomon: "I will be his father, and he shall be my son" (II Sam. 7:14). Moreover, the Second Psalm, evidently part of a coronation ritual for the king in Jerusalem, declares that the Lord says to "his anointed" (that is, his "messiah" in Hebrew), "You are my son, today I have begotten you" (Ps. 2:7). Thus, the "messiah" was "begotten" as son of God on the day of his coronation. That such Jewish thinking lies behind some very early Christian conceptions of Jesus' sonship seems clear from the partial use of this psalm in the baptism scene, "Thou art my son" (Mark 1:11). But since all of our manuscripts of Mark's Gospel exclude the second line from Psalm 2:7 ("today I have begotten you"), it is not clear whether Mark himself held this very early Jewish-Christian theology. Interestingly, however, other narratives about the baptism *do* quote all of Psalm 2:7. The gospel of the Ebionites, for example, reads:

> And as he came up from the water, the heavens were opened, and he saw the Holy Spirit descending in the form of a dove and entering into him. And a voice from heaven said, "Thou art my beloved Son; with thee I am well pleased." And again, "Today I have begotten thee."[8]

Similarly, the author of Hebrews, in chapter 1 verse 5, writes that God said of Jesus, "Thou art my Son, today I have begotten thee." The Ebionites appear to have held this "adoptionist" view of Jesus' divine sonship. Likewise, certain early manuscripts of Luke quote all of Psalm 2:7: Luke 3:22 in Codex Bezae, and certain Old Latin manuscripts used by Justin, Clement, Origen, and Augustine read, "Thou art my Son; today I have begotten thee."

Mark borrowed an already-created baptism episode, one unconcerned about the implications of Jesus' repented sins; it was at some point in its development "adoptionist" with regard to Jesus' sonship.

Mark's baptism scene puts Jesus in the tradition of the great prophets of the past who were inaugurated to a new role as Yahweh's spokesmen; it is modelled in part on the opening of Ezekiel's inaugural vision: "The heavens were opened and I saw a vision of God" (Ezek. 1:1). On its way to Mark, the scene was in turn mediated through the Testament of the Twelve Patriarchs:

> The heavens shall be opened
> And from the temple of glory shall come upon him sanctification
> With the Father's voice . . .
> And the glory of the Most High shall be uttered over him.
>
> (Levi 18:6)

Another of the Testaments provided an even more specific detail:

And the heavens shall be opened to him
To pour out the spirit, the blessing of the Holy Father.

(Judah 24:3)

The scene passed through partial development on its way to Mark, shedding its "adoptionist" theology but not yet losing its implication that Jesus was one among many repentant sinners.

Another embarrassment in Mark's inherited baptismal scene is John the Baptist himself. He clearly had a role in initiating Jesus' career, but the relationship was obviously troubling to some Christian minds, especially as Mark presents it. The mythical role of descending-ascending heavenly figure fits John in Mark's first chapter better than it fits Jesus! That is to say, Mark, or rather his Greek source, has presented John the Baptist as a kind of Elijah Redivivus or Elijah Reincarnate. Because of the last verses in the Old Testament, many in the first century expected that at the end time Elijah, who had gone up to heaven in a chariot of fire and was believed to be still there (II Kings 2:11), would return:

Look, I will send you the prophet Elijah before the great and terrible day of the LORD comes. He will reconcile fathers to sons and sons to fathers.

(Mal. 4:5-6)

The Gospel of Mark describes John the Baptist as this figure, picturing him in the Septuagint vocabulary used for Elijah: "John was dressed in a rough coat of camel's hair, with a leather belt [zōnēn dermatinēn] round his waist [peri tēn osphyn autou]" (Mark 1:6), just as Elijah is described as a "hairy man, girt with a leathern girdle [zōnēn dermatinēn] about his loins [tēn osphyn autou]" (IV [II] Kings 1:8 LXX). Thus the myth of the descending Elijah is present, at least implicitly, in the first chapter of Mark, but not the myth of the descending redeemer; Jesus becomes (or at least is announced as) the Son of God only at the baptism, and there is no hint in Mark's first chapter that Jesus was in any way the Son of God *before* his baptism; indeed, there is the clear hint that at least Mark's source, if not Mark himself, held the "adoptionist" theology. Now there is no reason to doubt that Mark believed in the preexistence of Jesus before he came to earth—indeed the Parable of the Vineyard in chapter 12 allegorically presents Jesus as God's "own dear son" sent to the vineyard of Israel—but Mark fails to give any account of how this preexistent son became the man Jesus: instead, he presents a clearer myth of a descending heavenly figure in Elijah/John than in Jesus.

All things considered, then, Mark does not begin his story of Jesus very satisfactorily. Indeed, within two or three decades of Mark's completion, there were at least two, and perhaps three, different writers (or Christian groups) who felt the need to produce an expanded and corrected version. Viewed from their perspective, the Gospel of Mark has some major shortcomings: It contains no birth narrative; it implies that Jesus, a repentant sinner, became the Son of God only at his baptism; it recounts no resurrection appearances; and it ends with the very unsatisfactory notion that the women who found the Empty Tomb were too afraid to speak to anyone about it. Moreover, Mark includes very little of Jesus' teachings; worse yet, (from Matthew's point of view) he even misunderstood totally the purpose of Jesus' use of parables. Indeed, by the last two decades of the first century, Mark's theology seemed already old-fashioned and even slightly suggestive of heresy. So, working apparently without knowledge of each other, within perhaps twenty or thirty years after Mark, two authors (or Christian groups), now known to us as "Matthew" and "Luke" (and even a third, in the view of some—"John") set about rewriting and correcting the first unsatisfactory Gospel. In their respective treatments of the baptism one obtains a good sense of their methods.

Perhaps the earliest revision of Mark is to be found in the Gospel of Matthew. Of the 661 verses in Mark, 606 appear in Matthew, many with deliberate stylistic and theological changes, others with fictional additions. One of the most obvious changes serves simple accuracy in, among other things, the use of Scripture. Whereas Mark introduces John the Baptist as follows:

> In the prophet Isaiah it stands written: "Here is my herald whom I send on ahead of you, and he will prepare your way. A voice crying aloud in the wilderness, 'Prepare a way for the Lord; clear a straight path for him,'"

Matthew introduces John thus:

> It is of him that the prophet Isaiah spoke when he said, "A voice crying aloud in the wilderness, 'Prepare a way for the Lord; clear a straight path for him.'"

Mark had used his source uncritically, not bothering to check its scriptural accuracy; but Matthew used *his* source—the Gospel of Mark—with a close critical eye, almost always checking its references to the Old Testament and changing them when necessary, in this case dropping the verse from Malachi wrongly attributed to Isaiah and keeping only what was truly Isaianic.

Matthew disliked Mark's perhaps careless implication that Jesus was just another repentant sinner, so he carefully tones it down, inventing a little dramatic scene: When Jesus

> came to John to be baptized by him, John tried to dissuade him. "Do you come to me?" he said; "I need rather to be baptized by you." Jesus replied, "Let it be so for the present; it is suitable to conform in this way with all that God requires." John then allowed him to come.
>
> (Matt. 3:13-15)

This scene is found in no other Gospel and indeed contains two words (*diekōluen,* "dissuade"; *prepon,* "suitable") found nowhere else in the New Testament. The verses are Matthew's own composition, created to deal with his unease at Mark's implication about the reason Jesus was baptized—not as a repentant sinner but to fulfill a divine requirement. Why God should require Jesus to be baptized, Matthew does not say.

Matthew was equally unhappy with the next sentences of Mark and proceeded to compose more fiction on the basis of them. Mark presents the scene as a private revelation to Jesus (italics added):

> At the moment when he came up out of the water, *he* saw the heavens torn open and the Spirit, like a dove, descending upon him. And a voice spoke from heaven: "*Thou* are my only Son, my Beloved; on *thee* my favour rests."
>
> (Mark 1:10-11)

Mark's scene could well be taken as revealing new information to Jesus, telling him, as the source of the line in Psalm 2 has it, that *at this moment* he was becoming God's Son. Matthew will have none of this, and re-creates the scene as a public revelation to the bystanders:

> After baptism Jesus came up out of the water at once, and at that moment heaven opened; he saw the Spirit of God descending like a dove to alight upon him; and a voice from heaven was heard saying, "This is my Son, my Beloved, on whom my favour rests."
>
> (Matt. 3:16-17)

Matthew delays the announcement until Jesus leaves the water of the Jordan (perhaps to separate him from John), allowing the focus of the scene to shift to the one baptized. There is no need, in Matthew, for Jesus to be told who he is, for he knows perfectly well; indeed, Matthew has already given the reader two chapters about Jesus' birth and divine parentage (see my chapter 3). It is not *Jesus* who needs to be told who he is, but everyone else. John apparently knew already, for he had attempted to dissuade Jesus from being (needlessly) baptized. How John knew, Matthew does not say; still, he has failed to look forward to his eleventh chapter, where John does *not* know who Jesus is, and sends disciples to ask, "Are you the one who is to come, or are we to expect some other [Matt.11:3]?" Here Matthew writes from a source other than Mark (one commonly called "Q," from the German *Quelle,* "source," which he shares with Luke) seemingly having temporarily forgotten his chapter-three fiction concerning John's certainty about Jesus' identity.

Like Matthew, Luke was also unhappy with Mark's account of the baptism and made, in his own way, similar changes. Like Matthew, he dropped Mark's uncritical attribution of Malachi to Isaiah. And like Matthew, he examined the text of Isaiah for Mark's quotation; there he found that two subsequent verses, ignored by both Matthew and Mark, suited his own themes perfectly, so he quoted them as well:

> The word of God came to John, son of Zechariah, in the wilderness. And he went all over the Jordan valley proclaiming a baptism in token of repentance for the forgiveness of sins, as it is written in the book of the prophecies of Isaiah:
> > "A Voice crying aloud in the wilderness,
> > 'Prepare a way for the Lord;
> > clear a straight path for him.
> > Every ravine shall be filled in,
> > and every mountain and hill levelled;
> > the corners shall be straightened,
> > and the rugged ways made smooth;
> > and all mankind shall see God's deliverance.'"
> >   (Luke 3:2-6)

Luke too has created a dramatic scene; the voice in the wilderness does not belong to John, as in Matthew and Mark, but to God,

telling John to "prepare a way for the Lord" (Jesus). Thus there
are two divine speeches in the wilderness, both of them inaugurations
of a special figure, the first sent as forerunner to the second. Luke
wanted the concept contained in Isaiah 40:5 included in his version
of the commission to John because it matched his central theme
of the universality of the Gospel, that it was for "all flesh." And
just as the speech to John from Isaiah was a commission, so the
speech to Jesus from the Psalm was one as well. But interestingly,
Luke also used Psalm 2:7 in a speech composed for Paul. In Paul's
theology, Jesus "was declared Son of God by a mighty act in
that he rose from the dead" (Rom. 1:4). Luke apparently knew
of this Pauline teaching for he has Paul quoting Psalm 2:7 as
a speech uttered to Jesus at his resurrection, not at his baptism:

> God, who made the promise to the fathers, has fulfilled it for the children
> by raising Jesus from the dead, as indeed it stands written in the second
> Psalm: "You are my son; this day I have begotten you."
>
> (Acts 13:32-33)

For Luke and Paul, Psalm 2:7 is a resurrection prophecy, not
a baptism prophecy. Thus, unlike Matthew, Luke has no qualms
about reproducing the divine speech at the baptism exactly as he
found it in Mark: "Thou art my Son, my Beloved; on thee my
favour rests" (Luke 3:22). Given his understanding of the Psalm,
Luke allowed the speech to follow his story of the birth of Jesus
in his first two chapters, which, like Matthew, argues that Jesus
is God's Son at least in part because God made his mother pregnant
(see my chapter 3). Nor is Luke embarrassed by Jesus' baptism
among other sinners.

The Fourth Gospel takes an extreme way of dealing with the
embarrassment of Jesus' baptism by John: you will find there no
statement that Jesus ever was baptised. In this Gospel John's purpose
is not to baptize Jesus but to proclaim him "the Lamb of God"
(John 1:29). Instead of presenting a baptism, the Fourth Gospel

turns the whole episode into a speech by the Baptist, avoiding
the question of Jesus' "repentance for the forgiveness of sins":

> I saw the Spirit coming down from heaven like a dove and resting
> upon him. I did not know him, but he who sent me to baptize in
> water told me, "When you see the spirit coming down upon someone
> and resting upon him, you will know that this is he who is to baptize
> in Holy Spirit." (John 1:32-33)

Matthew's embarrassed fiction that John, knowing already who
Jesus was, tried to dissuade him from baptism is obviated by the
Fourth Gospel's fictional creation of a scene of revelation. John
does not know who Jesus really is until he sees the dove that
God has told him to look for descending. The embarrassment in
the Fourth Gospel is of a different kind: in order to avoid mention
of Jesus' baptism, the fourth evangelist had to create four separate
implied scenes—John being told how to recognize Jesus, recognizing
him, proclaiming Jesus as the Lamb of God and then revealing
how he discovered Jesus' identity. The extraordinary awkwardness
of this sequence, compared to the simplicity (doctrinally
embarrassing though it be) of Mark's baptism scene, shows the
author's scenic ingenuity taxed to its limit by the felt necessity
to avoid depicting Jesus as a repentant sinner being baptized by
John.

Developing theology creates fictions; moreover, each gospel
implicitly argues the fictitiousness of the others. As R. Joseph
Hoffmann has put it, "Every gospel is tendentious in relation to
any other."[9] This is especially true with regard to Mark and the
Gospels—Matthew and Luke in particular—intended to render
Mark obsolete. The fictionalizing of Mark is one of the implicit
purposes of the First and Third Gospels, whose writers used what
were probably, in their communities, rare or even unique copies
of Mark and who clearly expected that no more would be heard
of Mark after their own Gospels were circulated. We do an injustice,

Hoffmann notes, "to the integrity of the Gospels when we imagine that these four ever intended to move into the same neighborhood."[10]

This becomes quite clear, for example, in two synoptic scenes describing Jesus' telling the parable of the sower and the seed:

> When he was alone, the Twelve and others who were round him questioned him about the parables. He replied, "To you the secret of the kingdom of God has been given; but to those who are outside, everything comes by way of parables, so that (as Scripture says) they may look and look, but see nothing; they may hear and hear, but understand nothing; otherwise they might turn to God and be forgiven." (Mark 4:10-12)

It is not difficult to imagine Matthew reading this passage, scratching his head, and wondering how Mark could so totally misunderstand the purpose of a parable—a small story intended to illuminate an idea, not obscure it. But Mark was a gentile, living perhaps in Rome; and though he clearly knew little of the tradition of Jewish rabbinic parabolic teaching, he was familiar with Greek allegorical writing, which was often used to present esoteric ideas in mystifying form. Matthew, on the other hand, was a Hellenistic Jewish Christian who knew perfectly well that a rabbi's parables were intended to elucidate, not obfuscate. Yet, here was Mark clearly insisting that Jesus' parables were meant to prevent people's understanding his message or being forgiven by God, a passage, moreover, that cites Scripture to prove its point. We can imagine Matthew's relief when he checked the reference in the Old Testament and found that Mark had got it wrong. Actually, Mark's citation of Isa. 6:9-10 agrees with the Aramaic version rather than with the Septuagint, but Matthew went to the latter for his quotation, which allowed him completely to change the point of Jesus' statement:

> The disciples went up to him and asked, "Why do you speak to them in parables?" He replied, "It has been granted to you to know the secrets of the kingdom of Heaven; but to those others it has not been granted.

> For the man who has will be given more, till he has enough and to spare; and the man who has not will forfeit even what he has. That is why I speak to them in parables; for they look without seeing, and listen without hearing or understanding. There is a prophecy of Isaiah which is being fulfilled for them: 'You may hear and hear, but you will never understand; you may look and look, but you will never see. For this people's mind has become gross; their ears are dulled, and their eyes are closed. Otherwise, their eyes might see, their ears hear, and their mind understand, and then they might turn again, and I would heal them.'" (Matt. 13:10-15)

Jesus speaks in parables to enhance people's understanding, insists Matthew, not to prevent it. That Mark's account of the scene is simply wrong is Matthew's implication.

Thus, Mark was as much a work of misguided fiction about the purpose of parables as it was about the baptism and the meaning of sonship. Indeed, the latter may be a major reason behind the need felt by Matthew and Luke to replace the Gospel of Mark: The earliest Gospel could easily play into the hands of those heretical Gnostic Christians who were teaching a Christology and notion of Jesus' sonship quite unacceptable to the orthodox tradition. They argued that the Son of God entered Jesus at baptism and left him before he died on the cross, as in the depiction of Jesus' death in the apocryphal Gospel of Peter:

> And the Lord cried out, saying, My power, my power, thou hast forsaken me. And when he had said it he was taken up. (5)

Matthew and Luke found that one way of dealing with the Sonship question lay in the nativity legends already circulating about Jesus: he was the Son of God because God impregnated his mother. Both Matthew and Luke added birth narratives to their revisions of Mark, basing them on legends quite irreconcilable with each other. The next chapter examines these nativity legends.

III

NATIVITY LEGENDS

Two of the four canonical Gospels—Matthew and Luke—give accounts of the conception and birth of Jesus. John tells us only of the Incarnation—that the Logos "became flesh"—while Mark says nothing at all about Jesus until his baptism as a man of perhaps thirty; either Mark and John know nothing about Jesus' background and birth, or they regard them as unremarkable. Certainly Mark, the earliest Gospel, knows nothing of the Annunciation or the Virgin Birth. It is clear from 3:20-21 that in Mark's view the conception of Jesus was accompanied by no angelic announcement to Mary that her son was to be (in Luke's words) "Son of the Most High" and possessor of the "throne of David" (Luke 1:32 NEB). According to Mark, after Jesus had openly declared himself Son of Man (a heavenly being, according to Daniel 7:13), his family on hearing of this "set out to take charge of him. 'He is out of his mind,' they said." Surely Jesus' mother and brothers

(so identified in Mark 3:31) would not have regarded Jesus' acts
as signs of insanity if Mark's Mary, like Luke's, had been told
by the angel Gabriel that her son would be the Messiah.

But Mark's ignorance of Jesus' conception, birth, and background was no hindrance to the first-century Christian imagination.
Very early among Jewish Christians, the need was felt to define
Jesus' ancestry. Jews looked for a messiah descended from David,
but Mark has Jesus explicitly deny that he is "David's son," and
was almost certainly correct in doing so, for Jesus was a Galileean
and of different nationality from the Judaean David. Mark, gentile
like his (perhaps Roman) Christian community, had no need of
a Davidic Christ:

> Jesus went on to say, as he taught in the temple, "How can the teachers
> of the law maintain that the Messiah is 'Son of David'? David himself
> said [in Psalm 110], when inspired by the Holy Spirit, "The Lord said
> to my Lord, 'Sit at my right hand until I put your enemies under your
> feet.' David himself calls him 'Lord'; how can he also be David's Son?"
> (Mark 12:35-37 NEB)

This passage looks very much like an early Christian polemic, using
a rather quibbling construction of a psalm to justify Jesus' messiahship despite his admitted lack of blood ties to David. Many
first-century Jewish Christians, however, did feel a need for a
Davidic messiah, and at least two separate groups responded by
producing Davidic genealogies for Jesus, both to a considerable
extent imaginary and each largely inconsistent with the other. One
of each was later appropriated by Matthew and Luke and repeated,
with minor but necessary changes, in their Gospels. Each genealogy
uses the Old Testament as its source of names until it stops supplying
them or until the supposed messianic line diverges from the biblical;
after that point Christian imaginations supplied two different lists
of ancestors for Jesus.

Matthew's genealogy traces, through the paternal line, the

ancestors of Joseph to show that Jesus Christ is "son of David" (1:1). This is not so surprising until Matthew insists that Joseph is not really Jesus' father: "It is by the Holy Spirit that she has conceived this child" (1:20). Why, to show that Jesus is "son of David," trace the ancestry of a man who is not his father? The obvious answer is that the list of names was constructed not by the author of Matthew but by earlier Jewish Christians who believed in all sincerity that Jesus had a human father; such Jewish Christians were perhaps the forebears of the group known in the second century as the Ebionites, to whom the Davidic ancestry of the messiah was essential and who believed, according to the second-century Christian, Justin Martyr, that Jesus was "the son of Joseph and Mary according to the ordinary course of human generation."[1] Certain ancient manuscripts of Matthew give some credence to this view. For. whereas the received text of Matt. 1:16 (dating from the fourth century) reads, "Jacob begat Joseph, the husband of Mary, who bore Jesus," the Sinaitic Syriac version, dating from the early fifth century, has it: "Jacob begat Joseph. Joseph, to whom was betrothed the virgin Mary, begat Jesus." Another ancient manuscript in the Vatican Library reads, "Jacob begat Joseph, and Joseph begat Jesus."[2]

Like Matthew, Luke traces the genealogy of Joseph back to David and beyond. But whereas in Matthew 1:14-15 Joseph is son of Jacob, son of Matthan, son of Eleazar, Luke 3:23 tells us that Joseph was "son of Heli, son of Matthat, son of Levi." The difference, to say the least, is remarkable; the two genealogies in fact diverge after David (c. 1000 B.C.) and do not again converge until Joseph. It is obvious that another Christian group, separate from the one supplying Matthew's list but feeling an equal need for a messiah descended from David, compiled its own genealogy, as imaginary as Matthew's in its last third. And like Matthew's genealogy, it traces the Davidic ancestry of the man who, Luke insists, is not Jesus' father anyway, and thus is rendered pointless.

Moreover, according to Luke's genealogy (3:23-31) there are

forty-one generations between David and Jesus; whereas according to Matthew's, there are but twenty-seven. Part of the difference stems from Matthew's remarkably careless treatment of his appropriated list of names. The genealogy which came to Matthew was based in part upon the second and third chapters of I Chronicles, which lists eighteen generations from David to Jeconiah: Matthew uses only fourteen of the names, dropping Ahaziah, Joash, Amaziah, and Jehoiakim. He does this because he thinks not in terms of what actually happened, but of what can be shown as fulfillment of a prophetic pattern: in fact the saying "This was to fulfill what the Lord declared through the prophet . . ." occurs fourteen times in his Gospel. After recording his altered list of names, Matthew (1:17) declares:

> There were thus fourteen generations in all from Abraham to David, fourteen from David until the deportation to Babylon, and fourteen from the deportation until the Messiah.

He had counted fourteen names from Abraham to David and thought he counted fourteen from Jechoniah to Jesus, and decided that this concidence of numbers must indicate a prophetic pattern. But in fact he found not fourteen names from David to Jechoniah, but eighteen; so Matthew took the simple expedient of changing Joram into the father of Azariah (though he was, in fact, the great-great-grandfather) and Josiah into the father of Jechoniah (though he was, in fact, his grandfather). But the pattern was illusory in the first place, and Matthew could have been spared his trouble had he more carefully counted the names in the third group when proposing the pattern; for it contains not fourteen names but only thirteen.

Fourteen was a significant number to Matthew because he thought, as did the author of the Book of Daniel, one of his favorite Old Testament sources, in terms of divine arithmetic. Daniel 9:24–27 had predicted that there would be a period of seventy weeks of years from the end of the Babylonian exile until the coming of the messiah. Knowing this, Matthew's numerical imagination clicked; not only will there be a certain number of weeks of years until the Christ, there will be a certain number of weeks of generations too. Fourteen equals two "weeks" of generations. Three two-week periods (14+14+14) equal six "weeks" of pre-Christian generations in the royal line of Israel; thus, with Jesus begins the seventh, the "sabbath" week of Jewish monarchical history—the kingdom, restored under Christ. Matthew included a genealogy not because he was really interested in the ancestry of Jesus— presumably he had the wits to grasp the pointlessness of tracing the genealogy of Joseph, who his own narrative denies is Jesus' father—but because he was interested in the pattern, the prophetic "fulfillment," even if he had to juggle the numbers to achieve it.

Thus we have a fascinating picture of four separate Christian communities in the first century. Two of them, Jewish-Christian, were determined to have a messiah with Davidic ancestry and constructed genealogies to prove it, never dreaming that Jesus could be thought of as having no human father. The other two, though interested in the possibility of Jesus' royal ancestry, were apparently content to do without it except in the merely legal sense (the legal but not actual father was Davidic). Far more important to them was what the title "Son of God" meant, and for them it implied actual divine paternity. Out of these latter two communities came our Gospels of Matthew and Luke.

Jews, and thus Jewish Christians, never had recounted myths of divine paternity of kings; their myths were "adoptionist." According to the Second Psalm, the "Lord's decree," addressed to each new king of Judah, was, "You are my son. . . . This day I have become your father." Jews had always read this in the obvious sense: on the day of his anointing, every Hebrew king became as a "son" to Yahweh. This notion goes back at least to the time of Solomon, when Yahweh was reported to have said, "I will be his father and he will be my son" (II Sam. 7:14). Actual divine paternity was, of course, not the issue here; there had already been a good deal of fuss over his father David's affair with Bathsheba, Solomon's mother. But gentile Christians in the first century, who came into the new religion directly from paganism and were already infected with myths about licentious deities, had a much different understanding of what divine paternity meant. Plutarch speaks for the entire ancient pagan world when he writes, in *Convivial Disputations,* "The fact of the intercourse of a male god with mortal women is conceded by all,"[3] though he admits that such relations might be spiritual, not carnal. Such mythology came with pagans converted to Christianity, and by the middle of the first century, Joseph's paternity of Jesus was being replaced by God's all over the gentile Christian world.

Of course, the new myth was not accepted everywhere. Jewish Christians, especially, regarded it as a pagan intrusion into their religion. In his *Dialogue with the Jew Trypho,* Justin Martyr concedes that some of his co-religionists reject the divine fathering and Virgin Birth of Jesus because they sound too much like pagan myth (Justin mentions the myth of Danaë, impregnated by Zeus): "It is quite true that some people of our kind acknowledge him to be Christ, but at the same time declare him to have been a man of men. I, however, cannot agree with them, and will not do so, even if the majority (of Christians) insist on this opinion." Justin's belief in the Virgin Birth is based, he says, upon "predictions set forth by the blessed prophets."[4] Obviously, Justin's view won out among Christians—another way of saying that Jewish Christianity virtually ceased to exist soon after the first century. The earliest statement in Christian literature of Justin's belief in the prophetic prediction of the Virgin Birth stands in the Gospel of Matthew (c. 80-100 A.D.) and is based on a typical first-century understanding of the Old Testament, specifically of Isaiah 7:14 in the Septuagint Greek translation of the Old Testament, the version used by most writers of the New. Matthew writes that Joseph, having learned of Mary's pregnancy after their betrothal, decided to have "the marriage contract set aside quietly" (Matthew was perhaps unaware that this was not possible under Jewish law; the process had to be legal and public). However,

> [an] angel of the Lord appeared to him in a dream. "Joseph son of David," said the angel, "do not be afraid to take Mary home with you as your wife. It is by the Holy Spirit that she has conceived this child. She will bear a son; and you shall give him the name Jesus, for he will save his people from their sins." All this happened in order to fulfill what the Lord declared through the prophet: "The virgin will conceive and bear a son, and he shall be called Emmanuel," a name which means "God is with us." (Matt. 1:20-23)

The Septuagint, from which Matthew quotes, uses, at Isaiah 7:14, *parthenos* (physical virgin) for the Hebrew *almah* (young woman) as well as the future tense, "will conceive," though Hebrew has no future tense as such; modern English translations are probably more accurate in reading (as does the New English Bible), "A young woman is with child." We can scarcely blame the author of Matthew for being misguided by his translation (though Jews frequently ridiculed early Christians for their dependence on the often-inaccurate Septuagint rather than the Hebrew); we can, however, fault him for reading Isaiah 7:14 quite without reference to its context—an interpretive method used by many in his time and ours, but a foolish one nonetheless. Any sensible reading of Isaiah, chapter seven, reveals its concern with the Syro-Israelite crisis of 734 B.C. (the history of which appears in I Kings 16:1-20): Isaiah's land of Judah has been invaded by Pekah, king of Israel, and Rezin, king of Syria. Isaiah approaches Judah's King Ahaz to assure him that the invasion will not succeed, and predicts:

> A young woman is with child, and she will bear a son, and will call him Immanuel. By the time that he has learnt to reject evil and choose good, he will be eating curds and honey; before that child has learnt to reject evil and choose good, desolation will come upon the land before whose two kings you cower now. (Isa. 7:14-16 NEB)

Isaiah obviously refers not to the circumstances of the child's conception but to his state a few years hence, the age of moral development;
before that time comes, says Isaiah, the invaders' lands will be desolate.
Actually, it was another thirteen years before Israel was conquered
by Assyria (721 B.C.); Isaiah was only approximately correct.

It is clear, however, that though the mistranslated and misunderstood passage in Isaiah was Matthew's biblical justification
for the Virgin Birth, it was not the source of the belief (indeed
Luke presents the Virgin Birth without reference to Isaiah). The
doctrine originated in the widespread pagan belief in the divine
conception upon various virgins of a number of mythic heroes
and famous persons in the ancient world, such as Plato, Alexander,
Perseus, Asclepius, and the Dioscuri. Diogenes Laertius's story,
in his biography of Plato, about Apollo's fathering the philosopher
upon Periktione, and its account of a dream granted by the god
to the woman's husband, may in fact have been a source of
Matthew's closely similar story:

> Ariston (the putative father of Plato) . . . had a vision in which Apollo
> appeared to him, and in consequence guarded her pure of the relations
> of wedlock until she brought forth Plato.[5]

Matthew writes that Joseph, having been similarly informed in
his dream, "had no intercourse with her until her son was born"
(Matt. 1:25).

Luke gives us a different myth about the conception of Jesus,
in which the Annunciation that the messiah is to be fathered by
God, not Joseph, is made to Mary rather than to her betrothed.
But Luke's account contains a strange anomaly:

> The angel Gabriel was sent from God to a town in Galilee called Nazareth,
> with a message for a girl betrothed to a man named Joseph, a descendant
> of David; the girl's name was Mary. . . . Then the angel said to her,
> "Do not be afraid, Mary, for God has been gracious to you; you shall

RANDEL HELMS 51

conceive and bear a son, and you shall give him the name Jesus. He will be great; he will bear the title 'Son of the Most High'; the Lord God will give him the throne of his ancestor David, and he will be king over Israel forever; his reign shall never end." "How can this be," said Mary, "since I know not a man?" (Luke 1:26-33 NEB)

Mary's question is very puzzling: why should a woman about to marry wonder at the notion that she will soon conceive? "How can this be, since I know not a man?" was not part of the Annunciation legend Luke appropriated; it was added, either by Luke or by a later hand, to stress the divine conception, for the story Luke inherited clearly assumed that Joseph was Jesus' father. Note its careful stress that Mary is "betrothed to a man named Joseph, a descendant of David," as prelude to the angel's declaration that Jesus will possess "the throne of his ancestor David." In this same chapter of Luke we learn that Mary, like her kinswoman Elizabeth, comes from a Levitical rather than a Davidic family; the royal ancestry *had* to be Joseph's. And clearly the stressing of Joseph's Davidic lineage in chapter one relates directly to the Davidic genealogy of Joseph in chapter three; David is Jesus' ancestor because he is Joseph's ancestor: Luke's inherited account can mean nothing else. Embarrassed by the story's clear implicit denial of the Virgin Birth notion, Luke or a later Christian inserted Mary's odd question, but the clumsy interpolation makes hash of Jesus' royal ancestry.

In due course, Jesus was born, growing up in Nazareth of Galilee, a nationality different from the Judaean inhabitants of Jerusalem and its near neighbor, Bethlehem. After Jesus' death, those of his followers interested in finding proof of his messiahship in the Old Testament worked a Christian reinterpretation of Micah 5:2 concerning the importance of Bethlehem as the birthplace of David and his dynasty:

> You, Bethlehem in Ephrathah, small as you are to be among Judah's
> clans, out of you shall come forth a governor for Israel, one whose
> roots are far back in the past, in days gone by.

That is, the one who restores the dynasty will have the same roots,
be of the same ancestry, as David of Bethlehem. Prophesying,
it would appear, during the Babylonian exile, Micah (or actually
a sixth-century B.C. interpolator whose words were included in
the book of the eighth-century B.C. prophet) hoped for the restoration of the Judaean monarchy destroyed in 586 B.C. Only Christians
have traditionally read this passage in Micah as a prediction of
a future birthplace rather than as a description of the origins of
the Davidic dynasty; we do not see multitudes of Jewish faithful
eagerly eyeing the village of Bethlehem for the birth of the Messiah:
remember the Jews' rejection of Jesus in John 7:27: "We know
where this man comes from, but when the Messiah appears, no
one is to know where he comes from." But since some first-century
Christians *did* read Micah 5:2 as a prediction of the birthplace
of Jesus, it became necessary to explain why he grew up in Nazareth,
in another country, rather than Bethlehem. At least two different
and mutually exclusive narratives explaining this were produced:
one appears in Matthew, the other in Luke. Matthew has it that
Mary and Joseph lived in Bethlehem when Jesus was born, and
continued there for about two years, fleeing then to Egypt; they
returned to Palestine only after Herod's death. For fear of Herod's
son, they did not resettle in Bethlehem, but moved rather to another
country, Galilee, finding a new home in Nazareth. Luke, on the
other hand, writes that Mary and apparently Joseph lived in
Nazareth, traveling to Bethlehem just before Jesus' birth to register
for a tax census. They left Bethlehem forty days later to visit the
temple in Jerusalem for the required ritual of the first-born, returning
then to their hometown of Nazareth. Examination of these two
irreconcilable accounts will give us a good picture of the creative
imaginations of Luke, Matthew, and their Christian sources.

In most of Matthew's Gospel, the major source of information
about Jesus is the Gospel of Mark (all but fifty-five of Mark's
verses appear in Matthew, either word-for-word or with deliberate
changes). But Mark says nothing about Jesus' birth. When one
favorite source fails him, Matthew inventively turns to another—
this time to the Old Testament, read with a particular interpretive
slant, and to oral tradition about Jesus, combining the two in
a noticeably uneasy way. We must remember that for the Christian
generation that produced our Gospels, the Bible consisted only
of what Christians now called the Old Testament, and a particular
version thereof, the Greek Septuagint. But before they wrote the
New Testament, Christians created another entirely new book, the
Old Testament, turning the Septuagint into a book about Jesus
by remarkably audacious and creative interpretation. Meanings it
had held for generations of Jews, its historical and poetic content
especially, ceased to exist; it became not a book about the past
but about its own future.

Of course, other groups such as the Qumran sect also read
the Bible oracularly, but Christians specialized this technique,
finding oracles about Jesus of Nazareth. If a passage in the Septuagint could be read as a prediction of an event in the life of
Jesus, then the event *must* have happened. Thus, if Micah were
understood to mean that the Messiah was to be born in Bethlehem,
then Jesus must have been born there, no matter what his real
hometown. But as it happens, the Bethlehem birth story, dependent
upon the Christian interpretation of Micah, and the magi-and-
star legend, dependent upon Hellenistic and Jewish oral tradition,
fit together very uneasily. The story of the magi ("astrologers" is
a more meaningful translation) says that "the star which they had
seen at its rising went ahead of them until it stopped above the
place where the child lay" (Matt. 2:9). But Matthew must connect
this with his separate fiction of the Bethlehem birth, so he has
the magi go to Jerusalem, "asking 'where is the child who is born
king of the Jews? We observed the rising of his star, and we have

come to pay him homage.' King Herod was greatly perturbed when he heard of this," because of course he regarded *himself* as king of the Jews. In answer to the question of the magi, Matthew, quoting Micah 5:2, has the "chief priests and lawyers of the Jewish people" inform them that "the Messiah is to be born" in Bethlehem. But then the star proceeds to guide the magi directly to the spot where Jesus lay. They did not *need* to go to Jerusalem to ask anybody; but Matthew must relate his two separate stories.

If the birth at Bethlehem is required by Micah 5:2, whence the star and the magi, the Slaughter of the Innocents, and the Flight into Egypt? We are dealing here with a rich mixture of legends, both Jewish and Graeco-Roman. The legend of the star probably arose in a Christian community influenced by the second-century B.C. Jewish apocryphal book, The Testament of the Twelve Patriarchs, which contains a supposed oracle of Levi that referred in the author's intention to John Hyrcanus, the second-century B.C. Maccabean priest:

> Then shall the Lord raise up a new priest,
> And to him all the words of the Lord shall be revealed;
> And he shall execute a righteous judgment upon the
>   earth for a multitude of days.
> And his star shall rise in heaven as of a king.[6]

Thus: "Where is the child who is born king of the Jews? We observed the rising of his star" (Matt. 2:2). But the Testament of Levi mentions no magi; these formed a floating and almost universal element in legends about the births of and homage to kings and heroes. As Cicero says of the birth of Alexander the Great in *De Divinatione:*

> Everybody knows that on the same night in which Olympias was delivered of Alexander the temple of Diana at Ephesus was burned, and that the magi began to cry out as the day was breaking: "Asia's deadly curse was born last night."[7]

When the eastern ruler Tiradates, whom Pliny calls a "magus,"
came to pay homage to Nero, "He had brought magi with him."[8]
Approaching the Caesar, "He knelt upon the ground, and with
arms crossed called him master and did obeisance," writes Dio
Cassius.[9] In Matthew, when the magi entered the presence of Jesus,
they "bowed to the ground in homage to him" (Matt. 2:11). And
not only Nero and Jesus received such honors; Suetonius writes
in his life of Augustus that when young Octavius Caesar was born,
"Publius Nigidius Figulus the astrologer, hearing at what hour the
child had been delivered, cried out, 'The ruler of the world is now
born.' Everyone believes this tale." In the same section of this work,
Suetonius adds that when Augustus entered the house of Theogenes
the astrologer, the man "rose and flung himself at his feet."[10]

The story of the Slaughter of the Innocents has an equally
complex origin. Again, Suetonius writes:

> According to Julius Marathus, a public portent warned the Roman
> people some months before Augustus's birth that Nature was making
> ready to provide them with a king; and this caused the Senate such
> consternation that they issued a decree which forbade the rearing of
> any male child for a whole year.[11]

Likewise, Matthew 2:16-18 says that Herod "gave orders for the
massacre of all children in Bethlehem and its neighbourhood, of
the age of two years or less," citing a strangely irrelevant passage
in Jeremiah as an oracle about the event:

> So were the words spoken through the prophet Jeremiah fulfilled: "A
> voice was heard in Rama [a village several miles north of Jerusalem,
> and far from Bethlehem], wailing and loud laments; it was Rachel weeping
> for her children, and refusing all consolation, because they were no
> more."

Matthew possessed the legend and found the oracle. But note the
following Jewish Midrash on the story of the birth of Abraham:

On the night when [Abraham] was born, Terah's friends, among whom
were councillors and soothsayers of Nimrod, were feasting in his house,
and on leaving late at night they observed a star which swallowed up
four other stars. . . . They forthwith hastened to Nimrod and said, "Of
a certainty a lad has been born who is destined to conquer this world
and the next."

On learning that Nimrod wanted to kill Abraham, his father "Terah
then went home and hid his son in a cave for three years."[12] This
Jewish legend, which is of course amazingly similar to Matthew's
account, is a fictional embellishment, as is Matthew's story, of
the Genesis and Exodus legends of the births of Abraham and
Moses, enlarged by combination with the story of Balaam in the
Book of Numbers. Indeed, there are direct verbal echoes of the
latter two in Matthew's Gospel.

Balaam, like the stargazers in the Jewish and Christian birth-
legends, is from Mesopotamia, "from the east" (the phrases in Num.
22:7 LXX and Matt. 2:1 are identical—*ap anatolon*). A well-known
astrologer and diviner of omens, he has been summoned by Balak,
king of Moab, who fears the Israelites, recent intruders into his
realm. In this as in all the stories descended from it, the king and
astrologers consult together concerning the newcomers into the realm
who threaten the ruler (Balak, Nimrod, Herod). In all the stories,
the astrologers point to a special star, symbol of the arrival of the
new force (Israel, Abraham, Jesus). Says Balaam: "A star shall rise
[*anatelei astron*] out of Jacob, a man shall spring out of Israel,
and shall crush the princes of Moab" (Num. 24:17 LXX). The
astrologers in Matthew likewise point to a star: "We observed the
rising of his star" (*ton astera en tē anotolē*—Matt. 2:2).

Now the source of the story of the king (Nimrod, Herod)
who wants to kill the infant leader of Israel (Abraham, Jesus)
shifts to the account of Moses in Exodus, the classic biblical legend
of the wicked king (Pharaoh) who wants to slay the new leader
of Israel (Moses). Indeed, the story of Moses in the Septuagint

provided Matthew with a direct verbal source for his story of the flight into Egypt. As Pharaoh wants to kill Moses, who then flees the country, so Herod wants to kill Jesus, who is then carried away by his parents. After a period of hiding for the hero in both stories, the wicked king dies:

> And the Lord said unto Moses in Midian, "Go, depart into Egypt, *for all that sought thy life are dead" (tethnēkasi gar pantes hoi zētountes sou tēn psychēn*—Ex. 4:19 LXX).

> When Herod died, behold, an angel of the Lord appeared in a dream to Joseph in Egypt, saying, "Rise, take the child and his mother, and go to the land of Israel, *for those who sought the child's life are dead" (tethnēkasin gar hoi zētountes tēn psychēn tou paidiou*—Matt. 2:20).

Of course, Moses flees *from* Egypt to Midian, while the Holy Family flees *to* Egypt through Midian. Why did Matthew not make the parallel exact by having his characters escape likewise to Midian in the Sinai Peninsula? The answer relates to Matthew's reading of another passage in the Old Testament: "This was to fulfill what the Lord has spoken by the prophet: 'Out of Egypt have I called my son'" (Matt. 2:15). If God said he called his son out of Egypt, then to Egypt Jesus must have gone. As the stories of Moses and Balaam had supplied the star, the basis for Herod's wrath, and the Holy Family's flight, so Hosea 11:1 was found to "predict" where they would flee and thence return:

> When Israel was a child I loved him,
>   and out of Egypt I called my son.
> The more I called them,
>   the more they went from me;
> they kept sacrificing to the Baals,
>   and burning incense to idols.

Hosea's outrage against Israel's stubborn idolatry despite Yahweh's loving concern and his saving act of the Exodus was taken out of its context by early Christians, who turned one line of a complaint about the present and the past into a prediction of the distant future.

So Joseph arose, "took mother and child with him, and came to the land of Israel" (Matt. 2:21), paralleling Moses who "took his wife and children, mounted them on an ass and set out" (Ex. 4:20). But Matthew now faced another problem, raised by his earlier solution to the difficulty of Jesus' Nazareth upbringing despite birth in Bethlehem. Though Matthew had Mary and Joseph living in Bethlehem for two years after Jesus' birth, he obviously could not continue to allow them to live there: how bring them to Nazareth? Matthew provides a forgetful angel, who must appear twice to Joseph. As has been said, the first time, the "angel of the Lord" merely informs Joseph that since those "who threatened the child's life are dead," he may take the Holy Family back "to the land of Israel." But the angel has forgotten to warn Joseph that Judaea is still too volatile for them:

> Hearing, however, that Archelaus had succeeded his father Herod as king of Judaea, [Joseph] was afraid to go there. And being warned by a dream, he withdrew to the region of Galilee; there he settled in a town called Nazareth. (Matt. 2:22-23)

But it isn't only the angel who has nodded; Matthew himself has apparently forgotten, if he ever knew, that *another* son of Herod, namely Antipas, was also in control of the province of Galilee; by Matthew's criterion, that province ought to be as dangerous as Judaea. Still, to Nazareth must he go, for "This was to fulfill the words spoken through the prophets: 'He shall be called a Nazarene'" (Matt. 2:23). There is, however, no such passage in all the Old Testament; Matthew had apparently vaguely heard that such a verse was in the "prophets," and since he really needed to get the Holy Family from the supposed birthplace to the known hometown, he reported the fulfillment but left the biblical reference unspecified.

Like Matthew, Luke faced the same problem of reconciling

known Nazarene upbringing with supposed Bethlehem birth. His solution, however, was entirely different, and even less convincing. Whereas Matthew has the Holy Family living in Bethlehem at the time of the birth and traveling later to Nazareth, Luke has them living in Nazareth and traveling to Bethlehem in the very last stages of Mary's pregnancy:

> In those days a decree was issued by the Emperor Augustus for a registration to be made throughout the Roman world. This was the first registration of its kind; it took place when Quirinius was governor of Syria. For this purpose everyone made his way to his own town; and so Joseph went up to Judaea from the town of Nazareth in Galilee, to register at the city of David, called Bethlehem, because he was of the house of David by descent; and with him went Mary who was betrothed to him. She was expecting a child, and while they were there the time came for her baby to be born. (Luke 2:1-6)

Though Luke 1:5 dates the birth of Jesus in the "days of Herod, king of Judaea," who died in 4 B.C., he wants the journey from Galilee to Bethlehem to have occurred in response to a census called when "Quirinius was governor of Syria." As historians know, "the one and only census conducted while Quirinius was legate in Syria affected only Judaea, not Galilee, and took place in A.D. 6-7, a good ten years after the death of Herod the Great."[13] In his anxiety to relate the Galilean upbringing with the supposed Bethlehem birth, Luke confused his facts. Indeed, Luke's anxiety has involved him in some real absurdities, like the needless ninety-mile journey of a woman in her last days of pregnancy—for it was the Davidic Joseph who supposedly had to be registered in the ancestral village, not the Levitical Mary. Worse yet, Luke has been forced to contrive a universal dislocation for a simple tax registration: who could imagine the efficient Romans requiring millions in the empire to journey scores or hundreds of miles to the villages of millennium-old ancestors merely to sign a tax form! Needless to say, no such event ever happened in the history of the Roman Empire, but Micah 5:2 must be fulfilled. Such thinking underlies Luke's narrative as much as it does Matthew's:

> She was expecting a child, and while they were there, the time came for her baby to be born, and she gave birth to a son, her first-born. She wrapped him in his swaddling-clothes, and laid him in a manger [*phatnē*], because there was no room for them to lodge in the house. (Luke 2:6-7 NEB)

Luke's community, like Matthew's, scoured the Old Testament for references that could be interpreted as predictions of Jesus. The manger was found in Isaiah 1:3 of the Septuagint: "The ox knows its owner, and the ass his master's manger [*phatnēn*]; but Israel does not know me, and the people has not regarded me."

Bethlehem had "no room" for its Savior, and Israel did not know him; only the lowly ox and ass first saw his glory. But it was a kingly role granted him from the first, for though Luke has no magi or gifts, as does Matthew's legend, he relates Jesus, through swaddling, to Solomon himself, who wrote according to the apocryphal Book of Wisdom (7:3-4 LXX) that "when I was born . . . I was nursed in swaddling clothes, and that with care. For there is no other king that had any other beginning of birth." Swaddled and placed in a manger, Jesus now fulfills these "predictions." That a manger or sheep-crib was a proper place for the new prince of Israel to be laid Luke felt certain, for had not the Lord said to David, "I took thee from the stables of the sheep, that thou shouldest be a prince over my people, over Israel" (II Samuel [II Kings] 7:8 LXX).

Thus for Luke the circumstances and place of Jesus' birth were not mere historical accidents; they were part of the prophetic "sign" of his royalty. As the angel says to the shepherds, "Today in the city of David a deliverer [*sōtēr*] has been born to you, Christ the Lord. And this is a sign for you, you will find a baby wrapped in his swaddling clothes, in a manger" (Luke 2:11-12 NEB).

IV

MIRACLES (I)
The Synoptic Narratives

Two conflicting attitudes toward miracles coexist in the Gospels: (1) faith causes miracles; (2) miracles cause faith. The first is the Synoptic view, the second the Johannine.

A main effort of the Synoptic miracle stories is to characterize Jesus as a compassionate wonder-worker: "When he came ashore, he saw a great crowd; and his heart went out to them, because they were like sheep without a shepherd" (Mark 6:34); "When the Lord saw [the widow of Nain], his heart went out to her, and he said, 'Weep no more'" (Luke 7:13). The first of these is part of the introduction to Mark's first account of the miracle of the loaves and fishes; the second, the introduction to Luke's story of the resurrection of the widow of Nain's son. Their characterizing function is obvious; their literary nature need no longer be in debate: They are fiction.

That the majority of the Gospel miracle stories are works of fiction is indeed no longer a vital question. As Ernest Käsemann writes:

> Over few subjects has there been such a bitter battle among the New Testament scholars of the last two centuries as over the miracle-stories of the Gospels. . . . We may say that today the battle is over, not perhaps as yet in the arena of church life, but certainly in the field of theological science. It has ended in the defeat of the concept of miracle which has been traditional in the church.

Käsemann's judgment is that the "great majority of the Gospel miracle stories must be regarded as legends." The kind of incidents which in fact commend themselves as being historically credible are "harmless episodes such as the healing of Peter's mother-in-law from a fever . . . [and] the healing of so-called possessed persons."[1] The next two chapters will examine the thirty-odd narratives in the Gospels which depict the Synoptic and Johannine attitudes toward miracles, demonstrate their literary lineage, and discuss how these fictional or legendary stories came to be composed.

Narratives about Jesus performing miracles were virtual requirements, given first-century Christianity's understanding of the Old Testament. Matthew 11:2–5 makes this quite clear:

> John, who was in prison, heard what Christ was doing, and sent his own disciples to him with this message: "Are you the one who is to come, or are we to expect some other?" Jesus answered, "Go and tell John what you hear and see: the blind recover their sight, the lame walk, the lepers are made clean, the deaf hear, the dead are raised to life, the poor are hearing the good news."

Matthew has Jesus list what are, in fact, signs of the advent of the New Age, as Isaiah had predicted: "The eyes of the blind shall be opened, and the ears of the deaf shall hear. Then shall the lame man leap as an hart" (Isa. 35:5 LXX). Earlier, Isaiah had also declared that "the dead shall rise, and they that are in the tombs shall be raised" (Isa. 26:19). With this, Matthew combined Second Isaiah's declaration that he had been appointed to "preach good news to the poor" (*euaggelisasthai ptōchois*—Isa. 61:1 LXX), using that prophet's very words from the Septuagint (*ptōchoi euaggelizontai*—11:5). Sayings taken as prophecies of Jesus' own time demanded fulfilling narratives.

As it happened, Scripture contained not only the prophecy, but the narratives as well; for the miracle stories about Elijah and Elisha in I and II Kings provided the basis for a number of the miracles attributed to Jesus. Remembering the principle that the early Christians turned the Old Testament into a book about Jesus, we can trace the literary lineage and grasp the literary structure of these stories. Both Elijah and Elisha, for example, mediate two striking miracles, the creation of abundance from little and the resurrection of a dead son. If these sound familiar to a reader of the Gospels, we should not be surprised.

The raising of a dead child or loved one is perhaps Jesus' most characteristic miracle. Lazarus (in John), Jairus' daughter (in the Synoptics), and the widow of Nain's son (in Luke) are all depicted as raised from the dead in order to present major themes of each of the evangelists.

Since Luke's account of the raising of the widow of Nain's son so clearly betrays its literary origins in the Septuagint, I shall begin with it:

And it came to pass [*kai egeneto*] afterwards that Jesus went to a town called Nain, accompanied by his disciples and a large crowd. As he approached the gate of the town he met a funeral. The dead man was the only son of his widowed mother; and many of the townspeople were there with her. When the Lord saw her his heart went out to her, and he said, "Weep no more." With that he stepped forward and laid his hand upon the bier; and the bearers halted. Then he spoke: "Young man, rise up!" The dead man sat up and began to speak; and Jesus gave him back to his mother. Deep awe fell upon them all, and they praised God. "A great prophet has arisen among us," they said. (Luke 7:11–16)

Either Luke or some Greek-speaking Christian behind Luke composed this story on the basis of the account in the Septuagint version of Kings depicting the raising of the dead son of the widow of Sarepta:

> And it came to pass [*kai egeneto*] that the word of the Lord came to Eliu, saying 'Arise, and go to Sarepta of the Sidonian land: behold, I have there commanded a widow-woman to maintain thee." And he arose and went to Sarepta, and came to the gate of the city. . . .
> And it came to pass afterward, that the son of the woman, the mistress of the house, was sick; and his sickness was very severe, until there was no breath left in him. . . .
> And Eliu said to the woman, "Give me thy son." And he took him out of her bosom. . . .
> And he breathed on the child thrice, and called on the Lord, and said, "O Lord, my God, let, I pray thee, the soul of this child return unto him." And it was so, and the child cried out, and he brought him down from the upper chamber into the house, and gave him to his mother. (III [I] Kings 17:8–10, 17, 19–23 LXX)

Both stories begin with a favorite Septuagintal formula, "And it came to pass." Both concern the dead son of a widow (*chē-ra*). In both the prophet "went" (*eporeuthē*) to the town, where he met the woman at the "gate of the city" (*ton pylōna tēs poleōs*— LXX; *tē pylē tē poleōs*—Luke), even though archaeological study has shown that the village of Nain in Galilee never had a wall; Nain's fictional gate is there for literary reasons—Sarepta's gate transferred. In both stories the prophets speak and touch the dead son, who then rises and speaks. In both stories it is declared that the miracle certifies the prophet ("Behold, I know that thou art a man of God"—LXX; "A great prophet has arisen"—Luke). And both stories conclude with precisely the same words: "and he gave him to his mother" (*kai edōken auton tē mētri autou*).

It is clear that either Luke or his source consciously modeled the story set in Nain after the miracle at Sarepta; what is even more striking is that *all* the Gospel stories of Jesus' resurrecting a dead loved one are based on the resurrections in the Books of Kings. The processes culminating in this fact seem fairly easy to trace. Early Christians knew, on the basis of Isaiah 26:19, that raising of the dead was to be one of the signs of the advent of God's kingdom, an event they saw happening in the person and ministry of Jesus; they knew equally well that events portrayed in the Old Testament were not merely descriptions of the past, but typological foreshadowings of the future, namely of Jesus. The only Old Testament narratives of resurrection are in the stories of Elijah and Elisha. After that, it is not unimaginable to see the widow of Sarepta, bewailing an only son, as the widow of Nain, doing the same.

Though only Luke of the four evangelists knew the story of the widow of Nain, the early Christian understanding of the Old Testament demanded that other such stories be told of Jesus; thus, Matthew, Mark, and John also contain narratives about Jesus' resurrecting a dead loved one, stories related, like Luke's, to the book of Kings. The Synoptic version is the raising of Jairus's daughter; the Johannine, the raising of Lazarus. This chapter examines the former.

In IV (II) Kings of the Septuagint, the Shunnamite woman has an only son who sickens and dies. At this, she goes to the prophet Elisha, falling at his feet to entreat for her son; but Elisha's disciple, Giezi, tries to thrust her away. Elisha rebukes Giezi, allowing the woman to plead for her child's lost life. The prophet sends his disciple on ahead, to lay his staff on the child, then rises and goes with the distraught mother. On the way, Giezi returns to tell them that the child is dead indeed, "not awaked," or "not risen" (IV [II] Kings 4:31 LXX).

> And Elisaie went into the house, and, behold, the dead child was laid
> upon the bed. And Elisaie went into the house, and shut the door
> upon themselves, the two, and prayed to the Lord. . . . And he went
> up, and bowed himself on the child seven times; and the child opened
> his eyes. . . . And the woman went in, and fell at his feet, and did
> obeisance to the ground; and she took her son. (IV [II] Kings 4:32–
> 37 LXX)

In Mark 5, Matthew 9, and Luke 8, the president of an unnamed
synagogue, one Jairus (whose name, "He will awaken," betrays
the representative and fictional nature of the account), comes to
Jesus, like the Shunnamite woman to Elisha, "falls at his feet and
entreats him many times," saying, in both Mark and Luke, that
his only daughter was dying. In Matthew, to align more closely
with the story's Old Testament source—as is typical of the careful
and knowledgeable first evangelist—the child is already dead. At
this point all three Synoptics intercalate the story of the woman
with the issue of blood. After that miracle,

> while he was still speaking, a message came from the president's house,
> "Your daughter is dead; why trouble the Rabbi further?" But Jesus,
> overhearing the message as it was delivered, said to the president of
> the synagogue, "Do not be afraid; only have faith." (Mark 5:35–36)

The story stays close to the Old Testament original; in both, the
prophet, on the way to the child, receives the message that it is
dead, but continues resolutely. In both stories the prophet seeks
privacy for the miracle: "After turning all the others out, [Jesus]
took the child's father and mother and his own companions and
went in where the child was lying," just as Elisha shut the door
upon himself and the child. And in both, the prophet touches
the child and speaks, and the child awakes. In Mark, the parents
were "ecstatic with great ecstasy" (*exestēsan . . . ekstasei megalē*
—Mark 5:42); in Kings, the mother of the child is "ecstatic with
all this ecstasy" (*exestēsas . . . pasan tēn ekstasin tautēn*—IV Kings

4:31 LXX). Just as the widow of Nain's son began as the widow of Sarepta's son, so the daughter of Jairus began as the dead child at Shunnam.

Matthew had Jesus declare to John the Baptist's messengers not only the signs from Isaiah (the dead raised, the deaf and blind restored), but also that "lepers are made clean," a statement not in Isaiah, but an act of Elisha taken as typological of Jesus— the healing of the leprous Naaman. That Old Testament leper found his first Gospel antitype in Mark 1:40–44 with parallels in Matt. 8:1–4 and Luke 5:12–16:

> Once he was approached by a leper, who knelt before him begging his help. "If only you will," said the man, "you can cleanse me." Moved to compassion, Jesus stretched out his hand, touched him, and said, "Indeed I will; be clean again." The leprosy left him immediately, and he was clean. Then he dismissed him with this stern warning: "Be sure you say nothing to anybody. Go and show yourself to the priest, and make the offering laid down by Moses for your cleansing; that will certify the cure."

This story, Bultmann points out, comes from Palestinian Christianity, for "show yourself to the priest" could hardly relate to a Hellenistic environment.[2] This story is modeled after the Elisha and Elijah miracles in the Books of Kings. In these stories, as in Mark's, the suppliant approaches the prophet and kneels, making his plea for a miracle. The prophet speaks, touches the beseecher, and the miracle happens. The prophet then sends him away healed.

The other leprosy-healing story in the Gospels appears in Luke, a narrative composed, either by Luke or a Greek-speaking source, by combining the above account from Mark with the story in IV [II] Kings LXX of the curing of Naaman's leprosy. As Bultmann notes, "Mk. 1:40–45 has been transposed into an imaginary story, in which gratitude and ingratitude are depicted on one and the same dramatic canvas."[3]

In the course of his journey to Jerusalem, he was traveling through
the midst of Samaria and Galilee. As he was entering a village, he
was met by ten men with leprosy. They stood some way off and called
out to him, "Jesus, Master, take pity on us." When he saw them he
said, "Go and show yourselves to the priests"; and while they were
on their way, they were made clean. One of them, finding himself cured,
turned back praising God aloud. He threw himself down at Jesus' feet
and thanked him. And he was a Samaritan. At this Jesus said,"Were
not all ten cleansed? The other nine, where are they? Could none be
found to come back and give praise to God except this foreigner?"
And he said to the man, "Stand up and go on your way; your faith
has cured you." (Luke 17:11-19)

The opening of the pericope is clearly Luke's own invention; there
is no such place as the "midst of Samaria and Galilee" (*meson
Samarias kai Galilaias*). Luke needs to indicate that the ten lepers
could be either Galilean or Samaritan, people of two different
nations and religions. At least one of the ten is a Samaritan, and
clearly Luke or his source is composing partly on the basis of
Mark 1:44 (or a story similar to it), since what would a Samaritan
need with a Jewish priest? Based on both Mark and the Septuagint
account of the cleansing of the leprous Naaman by Elisha, the
story arose in a Greek-speaking Christian environment. In the Kings
version, the prophet tells Naaman to "go" (*poreutheis*) wash in
the Jordan and "be cleansed" (*katharistēsē*—IV [II] Kings 5:10
LXX), just as Jesus tells the ten lepers to "go" (*poreuthentes*) to
the priests, and they were cleansed (*ekatharisthēsan*). One of the
lepers "turned back" (*hypestrepsen*) after his cleansing to praise
God, just as Naaman "returned" (*epestrepse*) to Elisha to praise
God after his cleansing ("I know there is no God in all the earth,
save in Israel"—IV [II] Kings 5:15 LXX). The literary lineage of
the rest of Luke's story is likewise a combination of Mark and
Septuagint Kings. The cry of the lepers ("Jesus, Master, take pity
on us") comes from the cry of the blind man at Jericho ("Jesus,
take pity on me!"—Mark 10:47). Similarly, Jesus' response to the

blind man at Jericho, "Your faith has cured you" (Mark 10:52), has become the basis for Jesus' words to the leper. One more relationship clinches the connection of Luke's ten-lepers pericope to Mark's blind man at Jericho. It has long been known that Matthew (20:39–34) and Luke (18:35–43) got their story of the healing of the blind man at Jericho from Mark chapter ten. But whereas Mark 10:46 places the healing when Jesus "was leaving the town," Luke 18:35 places it when Jesus was "approaching" Jericho. Apparently Luke read his source correctly, despite what our copies of Mark say; for Luke's story of the lepers based on the Jericho pericope also places the miracle as Jesus was "entering" the village. It would seem, then, that Luke, or his source, constructed the narrative of the ten blind men on the basis of the stories of Elisha and Naaman and of the blind man at Jericho, forgetting in the process the irrelevance of a Jewish priest to a Samaritan ex-leper.

Early Christians rummaged not only the stories of Elijah and Elisha in the Septuagint Books of Kings, but other stories as well. Third Kings in the Septuagint tells of an unnamed man of God who healed the withered hand of King Jeroboam. The man of God had just prophesied against the king's altar at Bethel, at which Jeroboam "stretched forth his hand" (*exeteinen . . . tēn cheira autou*), commanding the arrest of the prophet. But at that moment "his hand withered" (*exēranthē hē cheir autou*). The king repentantly pleaded with the prophet to restore the withered hand; so the man of God entreated the Lord, "and he restored the king's hand" (III [I] Kings 13:4–6). This narrative became the basis for the pericope about Jesus' healing a man's withered hand on a sabbath (Matt. 12; Mk. 3; Lk. 6). The first Gospel fiction stemming from the story appears in Mark 3:5 and is based on a Greek-speaking Christian tradition: In synagogue, on a sabbath, Jesus encounters a man with a withered (*exērammenēn*) hand (*cheira*) (Matt. 12:10 changes "withered" to the adjectival *xēran*, making it closer to the Septuagint); Jesus then instructs him to "stretch out" his hand: and he "stretched [it] out [*exeteinen,* as in LXX], and his hand was restored."

But of course Jesus was not only to do what Elijah or Elisha did, but even greater things, for was not Elijah to come back as a forerunner of Jesus, to "prepare a way for the Lord"? Jesus must, therefore, perform miracles even they could not. Conversely, any stories that might have been composed on a faulty theological basis, which hinted at any sort of limitation in Jesus' power, had to be eliminated from the stock of miracle narratives. So we find parallel and related tendencies in the literary history of the Gospel miracles: (1) The miraculous element is heightened, and any hint of limitation in Jesus' power is removed; (2) there is an ongoing "novelizing" process, a fleshing out of the stories to make them more "realistic," "detailed," "believable."

The second of these is best observed in the case of Malchus's ear, at the arrest of Jesus:

> Then they seized him and held him fast. One of the bystanders drew his sword, and struck at the High Priest's servant, cutting off his ear. Then Jesus spoke: "Do you take me for a bandit, that you have come out with swords and cudgels to arrest me? Day after day I was within your reach as I taught in the temple, and you did not lay hands on me. But let the scriptures be fulfilled." (Mark 14:46–49)

Readers of Mark noticed that the High Priest's servant's loss of an ear-lobe (the "little ear," *ōtarion*), was part of the fulfillment of scripture, and that Jesus uncharacteristically made no effort to come to the aid of someone in pain, merely berating those arresting him. It was not long before readers of the Old Testament noted that Amos had "predicted" that a "shepherd" would rescue from the mouth of a lion "two legs or the lobe [*lobon*] of an ear" (Amos 3:12 LXX). Jesus must therefore have healed the ear, and by the time of the writing of Luke's Gospel, he does. We even learn which ear:

> And one of them struck at the High Priest's servant, cutting off his right ear. But Jesus answered, "Let them have their way." Then he touched the man's ear and healed him. (Luke 22:50–51)

Others noticed that the bystander with the sword was not identified, nor was the injured man. John's sources supplied this information: "Simon Peter drew the sword he was wearing and struck at the High Priest's servant, cutting off his right ear. (The servant's name was Malchus)" (John 18:10).

The other process, the heightening of the miraculous and the elimination of hints about the limitation of Jesus' power to work miracles, is evident in later treatments of Mark's account of Jesus at Nazareth. There in his own hometown, says Mark, he was not notably successful:

> Jesus said to them, "A prophet will always be held in honour except in his home town, and among his kinsmen and family." He could work no miracle there, except that he put his hands on a few sick people and healed them, and he was taken aback by their want of faith. (Mark 6:4–6)

Matthew, with a more "advanced" theology and a more fully deified Jesus, could not accept Mark's assertion, so he treated it as fiction, untrue; it was not that Jesus *could not* perform great miracles in the face of lack of faith in him, rather he *chose not* to do so: "He did not work many miracles there: such was their want of faith" (Matt. 13:58). Matthew's theology has been satisfied: Jesus' limitation of power has been eliminated; but in enlarging Jesus' power, Matthew has shrunk his compassion, making him retaliate against the ordinary human limitation of weak faith. The more "primitive" picture in Mark of Jesus as surprised and partially helpless against faithlessness is more attractive and beguiling, less hardhearted.

Bearing this in mind, we may more readily grasp why Matthew

and Luke chose to leave out altogether two of Mark's miracle stories. In the latter, Jesus is asked to heal a deaf mute:

> He took the man aside, away from the crowd, put his fingers into his [the man's] ears, spat, and touched his tongue. Then, looking up to heaven, he sighed, and said to him, "Ephphatha," which means, "Be opened." With that his ears were opened, and at the same time the impediment was removed and he spoke plainly. (Mark 7:33–35)

In the next chapter, Jesus is asked to cure a blind man:

> He spat on his eyes, and laid his hands upon him, and asked whether he could see any thing. The blind man's sight began to come back, and he said, "I see men; they look like trees, but they are walking about." Jesus laid his hands on his eyes again; he looked hard, and now he was cured so that he saw everything clearly. (Mark 8:23–25)

For Matthew and Luke, who eliminated both these stories from their revisions of Mark, the notion that Jesus needed any kind of ritual (magic word) or medicinal (spittle) help, or even that he needed a little time and repetition of the treatment, was unthinkable. But having got rid of these healings of the blind and deaf, Matthew and Luke had to supply their own accounts of such healings, in order to satisfy the prediction of Isa. 35:5. Both went to the same non-Markan source to fill the need. According to Luke 11:14–15:

> He was driving out a devil which was dumb; and when the devil came out, the dumb man began to speak. The people were astonished, but some of them said, "It is by Beelzebub prince of devils that he drives the devils out."

Matthew ensures his story replaces the two he removed from Mark by depicting the man as both mute *and* blind:

Then they brought him a man who was possessed; he was blind and dumb; and Jesus cured him, restoring both speech and sight. . . . But when the pharisees heard it, they said, "It is only by Beelzebub prince of devils that this man drives the devils out." (Matt. 12:22–24)

A miracle story grows here before our eyes, Luke's mute becoming mute and blind. This process of the fictional enhancement of a miracle story is perhaps best observed in the case of the cursing of the fig tree, a miracle story that began simply as a parable. Luke has the parable—probably the original version of the episode—but not the miracle; Mark and Matthew have the miracle but not the parable. This strange story began very simply:

A certain man had a fig tree growing in his vineyard; and he came [*elthen*) looking [*zētōn*] for fruit [*karpon*] on it, but found none [*oukh heuren*]. So he said to the vinedresser, "Look here! For the last three years I have come looking for fruit on this fig tree without finding any. Cut it down. Why should it go on using up the soil?" (Luke 13:6–7)

In the oral tradition behind Mark, the man looking for fruit became Jesus, and the order to cut it down became his curse upon the tree:

Noticing a fig tree in leaf, he went [*ēlthen*] to see if he could find anything on it. But when he came there he found nothing [*ouden heuren*] but leaves; for it was not the season for figs. He said to the tree,"May no one ever again eat fruit [*karpon*] from you!" . . . Early next morning, as they passed by, they saw that the fig tree had withered from the roots up. (Mark 11:13, 14, 20)

Matthew takes the story from Mark, but his treatment is characteristic of what he does to that source—he fictionally heightens the miraculous and suppresses anything not in keeping with his theological understanding of Jesus:

> Seeing a fig tree at the roadside he went up to it but found nothing
> on it but leaves. He said to the tree, "You shall never bear fruit any
> more!"; and the tree withered away at once. (Matt. 21:19–20)

Matthew suppresses the part of Mark's account that makes Jesus look childishly petulant; also, he moves the tree to the roadside, so that Jesus with his supernatural knowledge will not unknowingly make a needless trip to gather fruit from a non-bearing tree. And since Matthew characteristically depicts Jesus' miracle-working powers as instantaneous, he makes that fictional change too. A parable becomes an even more striking miracle story.

Another form of fictional heightening of the miraculous takes place in the distance healing of the centurion's servant—the other miracle story common to Matthew and Luke but not found in Mark. In II Kings, a woman approaches Elisha to entreat him concerning her dead son. Elisha sends his servant to lay his (Elisha's) staff on the boy's face, but the child does not revive. Elisha, unable to perform a miracle at a distance, must go personally to perform it. The new story, told in Matthew and Luke, opens with the typical pattern of the Books of Kings. The prophet (Jesus) is approached and entreated to perform a healing (of the centurion's servant). The prophet agrees and sets out; the words are the same in Luke (who usually sticks more closely to the vocabulary of his source than does Matthew) and LXX: "Jesus went (*eporeuto*) with them" (Luke 7:6); Elisha "went (*eporeuthē*) with her" (IV Kings 4:30 LXX). In both stories the prophet receives a message while on his way to the boy: in the Old Testament, it is that the child has not revived, is indeed dead (the miracle at a distance has not worked); in the New, the message is one of faith that Jesus *can* work a miracle at a distance. Jesus is moved by the message ("Not even in Israel have I found such great faith"—Luke 7:9); "And the boy was healed in that hour" (Matt. 8:13). The oral tradition, using the miracle story pattern found in the Books of Kings, presents Jesus doing what Elisha could not.

Mention of the cursing of the fig tree brings us to the other so-called nature miracles, acts showing Jesus' lordly power over the world he and his Father had created: the feeding of the crowds of four and five thousand, stilling the storm, walking on the Sea of Galilee. Like so many of the other miracle stories, these too have their origins in the Old Testament.

Indeed, the Elijah/Elisha stories were thoroughly probed by first-century Christians; for the miraculous increase of food miracle common to their narratives, and invented by oral tradition, served as a source for two versions of a story about Jesus feeding the multitudes—Mark knew both narratives and treated them as two separate incidents. In the first of the stories used by Mark, Jesus feeds five thousand persons with five loaves and two fishes. Two chapters later Jesus and his disciples are again·in the wilderness, this time with four thousand hungry persons and only four loaves and a few fishes among them. The disciples, though they have presumably just witnessed Jesus feed five thousand with five loaves, naively ask, "How can anyone provide all these people with bread in this lonely place?"—Mk. 8:14. Mark obviously found the two stories in unrelated layers of oral tradition and, failing to grasp that they were different versions of the same story, put them into narrative sequence, making the disciples appear unbelievably stupid, either inadvertently, perhaps, or more likely deliberately, in order to point up one of his favorite themes: the consistently blind failure of the disciples to grasp Jesus' true nature.

In any event, both narratives stem from IV [II] Kings 4:42–44 read as a typological foreshadowing of the career of Jesus. Both Testaments specify the number of hungry persons (one hundred in the Old; four and five thousand—much greater miracles!—in the New); both specify the inadequate amount of food available (twenty loaves in the Old Testament; five and four loaves—again greater miracles—in the New). In both the prophets instruct their disciples to feed the people, and in both the disciples protest the inadequacy: Elisha's disciple complains, "I cannot set this before a hundred men" (IV [II] Kings 4:43); while Jesus' disciple asks, "How can anyone provide all these people with bread?" (Mark 8:5). Finally, in both stories, the meager loaves are miraculously amplifed to feed all present and more: "And they ate, and left some over" (IV [II] Kings 4:44); "They all ate to their heart's content, and seven baskets were filled with the scraps that were left" (Mark 8:9). The Elisha version apparently appealed to early Christians more than its companion story of Elijah providing a jar of flour and flasks of oil that were never to run empty (III [I] Kings 17); at least no stories based on this narrative entered the Synoptics.

Interestingly, the miracle of the loaves and fishes is one of only very few Synoptic miracle stories which have also been used in the Fourth Gospel; John's version at 6:9, in which a "boy" (*paidarion*) holds five loaves of barley (*artous krithinous*) reveals even more clearly than does Mark its source in Septuagint IV Kings, where the "boy" (*paidarion*) of Elisha, Giezi, is given some twenty barley loaves (*artous krithinous*) to feed a hundred men (IV [II] Kings 4:41–42 LXX). In Mark's account, the disciples possess the loaves of bread.

Jesus also showed his power over nature in fictions about water. The ancients knew from Psalm 107 what power Yahweh has over the sea:

> At his command the storm-wind rose
>> and lifted the waves high.
> Carried up to heaven, plunged down to the depths,
>> tossed to and fro in peril,
> they reeled and staggered like drunken men,
>> and their seamanship was all in vain.
> So they cried to the LORD in their trouble,
>> and he brought them out of their distress.
> The storm sank to a murmur
>> and the waves of the sea were stilled.
> They were glad then that all was calm,
>> as he guided them to the harbour they desired.
>> (Ps. 107:25–30)

From this famous and imaginative passage we can trace the fruitful development of three separate fictional, narratives, one of Jonah, two of Jesus.

When the author of the Book of Jonah was writing his story about the stilling of a storm, he consulted this Psalm for details. In Jonah 1:4, the Lord sends a great storm and a high sea; in the Psalm, at Yahweh's command, ". . . the storm-wind rose and lifted the waves high." Jonah's sailors "rowed hard to put back to land, but in vain" (1:13), and in the Psalm, "their seamanship was all in vain." In Jonah, the sailors "called on the LORD and said, 'O LORD, do not let us perish'" (1:14); in the Psalm, "They cried to the LORD in their trouble." As a consequence, Jonah says, the "sea stopped raging" (1:15); the psalmist, "the storm sank to a murmur, and the waves of the sea were stilled." In Jonah, the "crew were filled with the fear of the LORD and offered sacrifice and made vows to him" (1:16); in the Psalm, those saved from the storm are advised to "offer sacrifice of thanksgiving."

Early Christians regarded the career of Jonah as a type, a prefiguring, of the career of Jesus. As Matthew puts it, Jesus' generation would be given the "sign of the prophet Jonah"; for as "Jonah was in the sea-monster's belly for three days and three nights, . . . in the same way, the Son of Man will be three days and three nights in the bowels of the earth" (Matt. 12:39–40). Moreover, if the Lord stilled the sea in the case of Jonah, the same must happen in the case of Jesus. The account was written by Mark who received it from a Greek-speaking Christian tradition and did not seem aware of its source in the Book of Jonah. In it, we find Jesus' disciples ferrying him across the Sea of Galilee in an open fishing boat:

A heavy squall came up and the waves broke over the boat until it was all but swamped. Now he was in the stern asleep on a cushion; they roused him and said, "Master, we are perishing! Do you not care?" He awoke, rebuked the wind, and said to the sea, "Hush! Be still!"

The wind dropped and there was a dead calm. He said to them, "Why are you such cowards? Have you no faith even now?" They were awestruck and said to one another, "Who can this be? Even the wind and the sea obey him." (Mark 4:37-41)

Either Mark or his source was aware of this story's relationship to the Psalms, if not to Jonah, for Jesus' "rebuke" of the sea is made in similar vocabulary: *epetimēsen*—Mark 4:38; *epetimēse*—Ps.105:9 LXX. Though we cannot be sure whether Mark regarded his story of the stilling of the storm as prefigured in the Old Testament, it is quite clear that Matthew did, for he rewrote Mark's account, deliberately changing its vocabulary to align it with the language of the Septuagint "predictions."

Matthew's first clue came from the statement in Mark that Jesus "rebuked" the sea. Familiar with the Septuagint Psalms, Matthew went to the source of this remark and elaborated with it as guide. Whereas Mark had written that the waves "broke over [*epeballen*] the boat until it was all but swamped [*gemizesthai*] by the waves," Matthew, knowing that in the very Psalm in which the Lord rebuked the Red Sea, the water "covered" (*ekalypsen*) the Egyptians, preferred to say that the boat was being "covered [*kalyptesthai*] by the waves" (8:24). And just as the Lord's mighty acts were seen as "wonders" (*thaumasia*), Matthew 8:27 used the same verb form to say that the disciples "wondered" (*ethaumasan*) at Jesus' acts (Ps. 105:7 LXX).

Matthew also knew, unlike Mark, that the stilling of the storm was based in part on the Book of Jonah, for again he rewrote his version of Mark's narrative based on chapter one of Jonah, read as foreshadowing the story of Jesus. Because Matthew was unhappy with the disciples' rude remark to Jesus in Mark: "We are perishing! Do you not care?" he changed it into a prayer of faith: "Save us, Lord, we are perishing" (Matt. 8:25). Septuagint Jonah, the version used by Matthew, reveals the reason Matthew felt justified in changing Mark. Matthew recognized as a partial source of the disciples' "We perish [*apollumetha*]" in Mark 4:38, the speech of the sailors in Jonah 1:14 LXX: "Forbid it, Lord. Let us not perish [*mēdamōs, Kyrie. mē apolōmetha*]." But Matthew also observed that the ship's captain says to Jonah, "Call upon thy God, that God may save us, and we perish not [*hopōs diasō sē ho Theos hēmas, kai ou mē apolōmetha*]"—Jonah 1:6 LXX. Thus Matthew, taking key words from Jonah—"Lord," "save us," "we perish"—rewrites Mark: a fictional correction of a fictional account, each of which is based in its own way on the Old Testament.

With this in mind, the nature of the rest of the miracle story as Mark first wrote it is more easily grasped. If it seems strange that Jesus could sleep in the stern of a small open fishing-boat in the middle of a storm so violent that waves were breaking over the vessel and filling it with water, Jesus' sleep should be seen not as a description of an event but as a literary necessity, the fulfillment of a typological foreshadowing: "Jonah had gone down into a corner of the ship and was lying sound alseep when the captain came upon him." That the disciples should speak rudely to Jesus is likewise accounted for in the captain's speech: "What, sound asleep? . . . Get up" (Jonah 1:5-6). When Mark does not observe that the disciples were afraid during the storm, but only after the storm had been stilled, he is recounting an antitype, not an event, a literary fiction built from a supposed prefigurement: after the storm is stilled in Jonah, the men "feared [*ephobēthēsan*] the Lord with great fear [*phobō megalō*]"—1:6 LXX, just as in Mark, after the sea is calmed, the disciples "feared very greatly [*ephobēthēsan phobon megan*]"—4:41.

Jesus also showed his power over the sea by walking on it (Matt. 14; Mark 6; John 6); a variant of the stilling of the storm. Both versions reveal their origin in the same part of the Old Testament, Psalm 106 of the Septuagint (107 Heb.), with perhaps additional influence from the Book of Job. Early Christians knew from Job 9:8 that the Lord "walks on the sea [*peripatōn epi tēs thalassēs*] as on dry ground"; thus they also presented Jesus "walking upon the sea" (*peripatōn epi tēs thalassēs*"—Mark 6:48). But for the basis of their narrative about this "predicted" event, they went to the Septuagint Psalms, as may best be seen by comparing Mark's and John's versions of the pericope. The latter's account begins at 6:16: "At nightfall, his disciples went down to the sea [*katebēsan . . . epi tēn thalassan*] and got into their boat [*ploion*]," echoing the Septuagint: "They that go down to the sea in ships [*hoi kata-bainontes eis thalassan en ploios*] . . . these see the works of the Lord, his wonders in the deep" (Ps. 106 [107]:23–24 LXX). Mark 6:49–50 contains another echo of Psalm 106: When the disciples saw Jesus walking on the water they "cried out [*anekraxan*]," for "they were troubled [*etarachthēsan*]"; in the Psalm, those who go down to the sea in ships become "troubled (*etarachthēsan*)" in a storm and "cry [*ekechraxan*] to the Lord in their distress" (Ps. 106: 27–28 LXX). Their prayer brings deliverance, and the Lord "guides them to their desired haven" (v. 30), just as he does in John, where "immediately the boat was at the land to which they were going" (6:21).

   Matthew enriches his account with a fascinating addition about Peter's effort to copy his Lord. After the disciples recognize the figure on the water as Jesus, the impetuous

> Peter called to him: "Lord, if it is you, tell me to come to you over the water." "Come," said Jesus. Peter stepped down from the boat, and walked over the water to Jesus. But when he saw the strength of the gale he was seized with fear; and beginning to sink, he cried, "Save me, Lord." Jesus at once reached out and caught hold of him, and said, "Why did you hesitate? How little faith you have!" They then climbed into the boat; and the wind dropped. And the men in the boat fell at his feet, exclaiming, "Truly you are the Son of God." (Matt. 14:28–33)

Matthew's embellishment was probably borrowed from a Buddhist legend which appears to have made its way into the Christian oral tradition. One of the stories told by Buddhist missionaries, who were in Syria and Egypt as early as the second century B.C., similarly concerns the power of faith granted to a disciple of Buddha: A disciple who wanted

> to visit Buddha one evening . . . found that the ferry boat was missing from the bank of the river Aciravati. In faithful trust in Buddha he stepped into the water and went as if on dry land to the very middle of the stream. Then he came out of his contented meditation on Buddha in which he had lost himself, and saw the waves and was frightened, and his feet began to sink. But he forced himself to become wrapt in his meditation again and by its power he reached the far bank safely and reached his master.[4]

V
MIRACLES (II)
The Fourth Gospel

The Fourth Gospel presents an understanding of miracles quite different from that in the Synoptics, and even uses a word for miracle—sign (*sēmeion*)—which the others explicitly reject. In the first three Gospels, the miracles are evidence of Jesus' compassion and of people's faith. "When the Lord saw her, his heart went out to her, and he said, 'Weep no more,'" writes Luke of Jesus' encounter with the bereaved widow of Nain. Nowhere does John so introduce a miracle story. "My daughter, your faith has cured you," the Synoptic authors have Jesus say to the woman who suffered an issue of blood (Matt. 9; Mark 5; Luke 8). Mark 6:5 even claims (though Matthew and Luke refuse to repeat the verse) that in cases of weak faith, Jesus "could work no miracle." Nowhere in John is faith the precondition of miracle. In the Synoptics, faith precedes the miracle; in John, the miracle precedes faith, for Jesus' "signs" are those things by which he "revealed his glory [*doxan*] and led his disciples to believe in him" (John 2:11), *doxa* being the Septuagint word for the divine radiance, the glory of God, as in Isaiah 6:3. To see Jesus perform a miracle is to recognize his divinity; and for this reason John tells his miracle stories. Moreover, *not* to have seen Jesus in the flesh, and yet to believe in him, is even finer to John, who feels some ambivalence toward faith engendered by miracle: "Happy are those who never saw me and yet have found faith" (20:29); "Will none of you ever believe without seeing signs and portents?" (4:48). Indeed, the very word rejected by Mark's Jesus is the one chosen by John to symbolize Jesus' deeds: "He sighed deeply to himself and said, 'Why does this generation ask for a sign [*sēmeion*]? I tell you this: no sign shall be given to this generation'" (Mark 8:12). John's uneasiness about miracle-engendered faith, blending uncomfortably with the conviction that this was the way Jesus chose to reveal himself, may lie behind the strange fact that there are so *few* miracles in the Fourth Gospel: seven, compared to twenty in Matthew and twenty-one in Luke. John's way of accounting for the paucity of his miracle stories is to declare that he has written only a selection of a much larger number available to him:

> There were indeed many other signs [*sēmeia*] that Jesus performed in the presence of his disciples, which are not recorded in this book. Those here written have been recorded in order that you may hold the faith that Jesus is the Christ, the Son of God, and that through this faith you may possess life by his name. (John 20:30-31)

The present chapter will examine the following Johannine miracle stories: the water made wine at Cana (chapter 2); the healing of the nobleman's son (chapter 4); the healing of the crippled man at Jerusalem (chapter 5); the healing of the man born blind (chapter 9); and the supreme sign, the raising of Lazarus (chapter 11). A sixth story, the miraculous draught of fishes (chapter 21) is generally accepted as a later addition (along with the rest of the chapter) and seems a version of a story in Luke 5. Another sign, the feeding of the five thousand, was discussed in the preceding chapter.

The understanding of "signs" in the Fourth Gospel, indeed the word itself, stems from the Septuagint: Moses "wrought the signs [sēmeia] before the people. And the people believed" (Ex. 4:30-31 LXX). Moses' signs were transformations—a staff into a serpent and back again, his clean hand to leprous and back again, water into blood—all meant to engender belief:

> "Now," said the LORD, "if they do not believe you and do not accept the evidence of the first sign, they may accept the evidence of the second. But if they are not convinced even by these two signs, and will not accept what you say, then fetch some water from the Nile and pour it out on the dry ground, and the water you take from the Nile will turn to blood." (Ex. 4:8-9)

This is part of the biblical background for Jesus' first sign; as Moses was to transform water, so was Jesus, and for the same reason:

> On the third day there was a wedding in Cana-in-Galilee. The mother of Jesus was there, and Jesus and his disciples were guests also. The wine gave out, so Jesus' mother said to him, "They have no wine left." He answered, "Woman, what have I to do with you? My hour is not yet come." His mother said to the servants, "Do whatever he tells you." There were six stone water-jars standing near, of the kind used for Jewish rites of purification; each held from twenty to thirty gallons. Jesus said to the servants, "Fill the jars with water," and they filled them to the brim. "Now draw some off," he ordered, "and take it to the steward of the feast"; and they did so. The steward tasted the water now turned to wine, not knowing its source; though the servants who had drawn the water knew. He hailed the bridegroom and said, "Everyone serves the best wine first, and waits until the guests have drunk freely before serving the poorer sort; but you have kept the best wine until now."
>
> This deed at Cana-in-Galilee is the first of the signs by which Jesus revealed his glory and led his disciples to believe in him. (John 2:1-11)

Although the meaning of John's story stems from the account of
Moses quoted above, it also relates to a characteristic act of Elijah
and Elisha in the Books of Kings, the miraculous provision of food
discussed previously. An examination of the account of Elijah's
providing flour and oil in III Kings LXX reveals some direct verbal
sources for the story of Jesus' miracle at Cana. One of the most
puzzling aspects of this first miracle in the Fourth Gospel is Jesus'
rudeness to his mother: "Woman, what have I to do with you?
[*Ti emoi kai soi, gunai*]." As has been seen before, the statement
is here not a historical report but an antitype of Elijah: for the
woman (*gunē*) in need of food says to that prophet, "What have
I to do with thee? [*ti emoi kai soi*]" (III [I] Kings 17:18 LXX).
In both stories the prophet instructs those in need of sustenance
to take empty pitchers (*hydria*, LXX; *hydriai*, John) and remove
from them the needed provision, which miraculously appears. This
and the succeeding miracle in Kings, Elijah's resurrecting of the
woman's son, lead her to place her faith in him as a prophet: "I
know that thou art a man of God" (III Kings 17:24 LXX), just
as Jesus' act leads his disciples to put their faith in him.

But as it happens, Elijah's miracle provides flour, not wine.
Why the change? It appears that this miracle story in the Fourth
Gospel was not only mediated through the story of Moses, where
it picked up the concept of "sign," before it reached John; it also
went through one other transformation, influenced by the mythology of Dionysus. As Bultmann has pointed out:

> On the festival day of Dionysos the temple springs at Andros and Teos
> were supposed every year to yield wine instead of water. In Elis on
> the eve of the feast, three empty pitchers were put into the temple and
> in the morning they were full of wine.[1]

In other words this miracle story had an extensive history before
it reached the author of the Fourth Gospel. Neither he nor anyone
he knew attended a wedding at Cana-in-Galilee at which Jesus

provided a hundred and twenty gallons of wine to those who had already drunk so freely they had exhausted the day's provisions; the story is fiction and has a clearly traceable literary lineage.

Jesus also performs his "second sign" (John 4:54) at Cana-in-Galilee, but, as in Matthew 8 and Luke 7 (the healing of the centurion's servant at Capernaum), the miracle is performed at a distance, for the one healed, the nobleman's son, lies also in Capernaum. This Johannine story is, in other words, related to the two synoptic miracles (all set at Capernaum, all healings, at a distance, of a gentile), but it clearly is not directly descended from them. The story has a complex lineage, and appears closely related to a well-known Jewish miracle narrative. Compare the following scenarios:

> Once again he visited Cana-in-Galilee, where he had turned the water into wine. An officer in the royal service was there, whose son was lying ill at Capernaum. When he heard that Jesus had come from Judaea into Galilee, he came to him and begged him to go down and cure his son, who was at the point of death. Jesus said to him, "Will none of you ever believe without seeing signs and portents?" The officer pleaded with him, "Sir, come down before my boy dies." Then Jesus said, "Return home; your son will live." The man believed what Jesus said and started for home. When he was on his way down his servants met him with the news, "Your boy is going to live." So he asked them what time it was when he began to recover. They said, "Yesterday at one in the afternoon the fever left him." The father noted that this was the exact time when Jesus had said to him, "Your son will live," and he and all his household became believers.
>
> This was now the second sign which Jesus performed after coming down from Judaea into Galilee. (John 4:46-54)

> Once a son of Rabban Gamaliel (II) was ill. He sent two disciples to R. Hanina b. Dosa, that he might pray for mercy for him. When he (b. Dosa) saw them, he went up into the attic and implored mercy for him. When he came down he said to them, "Go, for the fever has left him." They said to him, "Are you a prophet then?". . . They returned and noted the hour in writing. When they came back to Rabban

Gamiliel he said to them: "By the Temple service!. . . It happened exactly
so in that hour the fever left him and he asked for water to drink."[2]

All these stories, the Synoptic, the Johannine and the rabbinical,
ultimately go back to the Elijah cycle in I Kings. Note in the rabbinical narrative the disciples sent as emissary, the healer seeking
privacy for his intercession, and the healing as a prophetic certi-
fication, all as in I Kings. Note in the New Testament stories the
healing at a distance and the recovery in the very hour the intercession was made, just as in the rabbinical story. Many traditions
grew from I Kings. Note particularly the very close verbal parallels
between John's story of Jesus and the narrative about Rabban
ben Dosa. R. Hanina says to the disciples of Gamiliel, "Go" (as
does Jesus to the boy's father—John 4:50), "for the fever has left
him" (just as John writes, "at the seventh hour the fever left him"—
John 4:52). Gamaliel says, "It happened exactly so in that hour,"
just as "the father knew that it was in that very hour that Jesus
spoke to him" the fever left his son (John 4:53). This kind of
fictional healing story was common in the first centuries of our
era, both in Jewish and Christian circles, and could be equally
applied to Rabbi Jesus or to another rabbi.

The next Johannine miracle story, Jesus' healing of the crippled
man at the pool of Bethesda, has a similarly complex history and
reveals more clearly the compositional methods of the author of
the Fourth Gospel. The first two miracles (water into wine and
the healing of the nobleman's son), both explicitly called "signs"
and both set at Cana, are widely taken to be from the same "signs
source"[3] and show little indication of large-scale alteration or
expansion by John. Neither miracle is followed by revelatory
discourse by Jesus; rather the two signs serve as introduction to
Jesus' ministry and gain for him a set of disciples: they "revealed
his glory and led his disciples to believe in him." Succeeding miracles,
however, are not listed as numbered signs, and are associated with
revelation discourses—the crippled man ("the Son gives life to men"),

the loaves and fishes ("I am the bread of life"), the man born blind ("I am the light of the world"), and the resurrection of Lazarus ("I am the resurrection and I am life"). The stories come, in other words, probably not from any written "signs source" but rather from the same kind of oral tradition behind many of the synoptic miracles and are based, like them, on Old Testament narratives. John then uses them as occasions for the discourses.

This is certainly the case with the story of the Samaritan woman at the well, which is not a healing miracle, though it does present Jesus as having supernatural knowledge. This narrative serves as the introduction to, and first occasion for, Jesus' announcement: "I am (the Messiah)" (John 4:26). It is a variant or altered retelling of the story of Elijah's meeting with the widow of Sarepta, itself a variant of what Robert Alter has called an Old Testament "type-scene"—the meeting of the hero with a woman at a well, of which he gives as examples the meeting of Abraham's servant with Rebekah (Gen. 24), of Jacob with Rachel (Gen. 29), of Moses with Zipporah (Ex. 2), and offers as modifications of the pattern the meetings of Ruth and Boaz (Ruth 2) and Saul and the girls at Zuph (I Sam. 9).[4] In such scenes, the young hero leaves his own land and journeys to a foreign country. There at a well he meets a woman (or women); water is requested and drawn from the well; the girl rushes home to bring the news of the young man's arrival; finally, a betrothal is arranged (p. 52).

Alter does not observe that another variation of the scene occurs in I Kings, the story of Elijah's meeting with the widow of Sarepta, a story repeated, in much of its essence, in John 4. In both stories the hero has left his own land and entered foreign territory (Elijah to Sidon; Jesus to Samaria). Both heroes are thirsty, and both ask a woman for a drink. In both stories the woman has no husband (though she is not a young nubile girl as in the type-scene: in I Kings she is a widow; in John a woman who has had five husbands and is cohabiting with a sixth man not her husband). Both heroes lack a drinking vessel and ask the woman for a drink from hers. But in both narratives, it is the *woman* who is truly in need of food or drink from the prophet, not vice-versa. Both prophets then promise the woman an unending source (Elijah, a pitcher of meal that "shall not fail" and a cruse of oil that "shall not diminish"; Jesus, a spring of water "always welling up for eternal life"—John 4:14). In both stories the woman expresses wonder that the prophet has called to mind her past deeds: "You came here to bring my sins to light" (I Kings 17:18); "He told me everything I ever did" (John 4:29). Subsequently, the woman in each story is moved to certify the prophet: "I know for certain that you are a man of God" (I Kings 17:24); "I can see that you are a prophet" (John 4:19). Although the Old Testament story has served as a source of the narrative in John, there are no direct verbal parallels between John's Greek and the Septuagint; we must assume that the story came to him from oral tradition or a written source dependent upon the Aramaic or Hebrew. John reworked the story, which originally seemed intended to show Jesus as having miraculous knowledge or insight (about the woman's serial marriages and nonmarriage) so that it became the introduction to an important discourse. We may observe the same kind of process at work in the story of the healing of the crippled man at the pool of Bethesda.

Apparently available to both Mark and John was an oral tradition concerning the Jewish leaders' opposition toward Jesus at least in part because he performed healings on the sabbath. Indeed, Mark confirms as much:

Again he entered the synagogue, and a man was there who had a withered hand. And they watched him, to see whether he would heal him on the sabbath, so that they might accuse him. And he said to the man who had the withered hand, "Come here." And he said to them, "Is it lawful on the sabbath to do good or to do harm, to save life or to kill?" But they were silent. And he looked around at them with anger, grieved at their hardness of heart, and said to the man, "Stretch out your hand." He stretched it out, and his hand was restored. The

Pharisees went out, and immediately held counsel with the Herodians
against him, how to destroy him. (Mark 3:1-6).

This story found its literary source in III (I) Kings 13 LXX, where
King Jeroboam is afflicted with a withered hand that is healed
at the word of a prophet:

> And it came to pass when king Jeroboam heard the words of the man
> of God who called on the altar that was in Bethel, that the king stretched
> forth his hand from the altar, saying, "Take hold of him." And, behold,
> his hand, which he stretched forth against him, withered, and he could
> not draw it back to himself . . . And king Jeroboam said to the man
> of God, "Intreat the Lord thy God, and let my hand be restored to
> me." And the man of God intreated the Lord, and he restored the
> king's hand to him, and it became as before.

Both stories use the same words—"withered" (*exērammenēn,* Mark;
exēranthē, Kings), and "stretched forth his hand" (*tēn cheira . . .
exeteinen,* Mark; *exeteinen. . . tēn cheira autou,* Kings). Moreover,
the activities of the prophet in both accounts led the authorities
to desire his arrest: Jeroboam ordered his men to seize the man
of God; the Pharisees and Herodians plotted together against Jesus.

Whereas in Mark, the plotting to destroy Jesus came in consequence of his sabbath-day healing of a withered *hand,* in the
Fourth Gospel the authorities plot against Jesus because of his
healing on the sabbath of a man with withered *legs,* a paralytic,

> crippled for thirty-five years. When Jesus saw him lying there and was
> aware that he had been ill a long time, he asked him, "Do you want
> to recover?" "Sir," he replied, "I have no one to put me in the pool
> when the water is disturbed, but while I am moving, someone else is
> in the pool before me." Jesus answered, "Rise to your feet, take up
> your bed and walk." The man recovered instantly, took up his stretcher,
> and began to walk. That day was a sabbath. (John 5:5-9)

According to John, "It was works of this kind done on the sabbath that stirred the Jews to persecute Jesus" (5:16). Mark's withered hand healed on the sabbath becomes John's withered legs healed on the sabbath, both leading to opposition to Jesus' works. That the oral tradition alters, develops, and blends narratives before they reach written form in the Gospels becomes even clearer when we note that John's story also relates to another narrative in Mark 2:9, the curing of a paralytic (*not* on the sabbath). There Jesus asks whether it is easier to say to the crippled man, "Your sins are forgiven," or to say, "Stand up, take your bed, and walk" *(Egeirou kai aron ton krabatton sou kai peripatei),* just as Jesus in John 5:8 says to the paralytic, "Stand up, take your bed, and walk" *(Egeire aron ton krabatton sou kai peripatei).*

That the blending of earlier narratives to form new stories occurred is clear from a passage in the apocryphal Acts of Pilate (6:2), which merges John's account of the healing of the man born blind with Mark's account in 10:46-52 in which a blind man cries out to Jesus:

> And another Jew came forward and said: "I was born blind: I heard words but saw no man's face: and as Jesus passed by I cried with a loud voice: 'Have mercy on me, O Son of David.' And he took pity on me and put his hands upon mine eyes and I received sight immediately."[5]

John's version of the healing of the congenitally blind man betrays yet another kind of source blending. In John's account Jesus made clay of his own spittle and anointed *(epechrisen)* the eyes of the blind man, who later says, "I saw again" *(aneblepsa)* (John 9:11). Such stories were not uncommon in the Hellenistic world, as may be seen from a Greek inscription probably praising the healing divinity Asclepius:

To Valerius Aper, a blind soldier, the god revealed that he should go
and take the blood of a white cock, together with honey, and rub them
into an eyesalve and anoint *(epichreisai)* his eyes three days. And he
received his sight *(aneblepse),* and came and gave thanks publicly to
the god.[6]

Although this kind of story lies behind John's, it does not account
for all of it; for like many of the Gospel miracle stories, this one
too is a variant or retelling of parts of the story of Elisha. It is
in IV [II] Kings, chapters 4 and 6, that the ultimate origins of
John's account of the healing of the blind man may be found,
which, before reaching John, may have been mediated through
something like the narrative of Asclepius quoted above. In the sixth
chapter of IV [II] Kings, certain men are made blind and then
given their sight again to serve God's purpose, just as in John 9:3
Jesus explains to his disciples that a man's blindness from birth
was so that "the works of God might be made manifest in him."
In the Old Testament story, "seeing" means both literal sight and
spiritual vision, for Elisha's servant is granted to see horses and
chariots of fire in IV [II] Kings 6:17; in John's story, the recovered
visual sense and newly gained spiritual insight (faith in Jesus) of
the once-blind man are contrasted with the spiritual blindness of
those who will not accept Jesus. Of those blinded in Kings, we
read in the Septuagint that the "Lord opened their eyes, and they
saw" *(diēnoixe Kurios tous ophthalmous autōn, kai eidon*—IV [II]
Kings 6:21 LXX), just as in John 9:17 it is said of Jesus that he
"opened" the eyes *(ēneōxen . . . tous ophthalmous)* of the man.
There is no mention of washing the eyes of the blind men in Kings;
but the direction by Jesus to the man born blind to wash his eyes
in the pool of Siloam made its way into John's pericope from the
story about Elisha in the preceding chapter of Kings. There, Naaman
the leper is told to wash himself in the Jordan to be cleansed of
his disease. Both healings have the same purpose: proof that "there
is a prophet *[Esti prophētēs]* in Israel" (IV [II] Kings 5:8 LXX)

and that Jesus "is a prophet [*prophētēs estin*]" (John 9:17). In both miracle stories, the one healed approaches the prophet and declares his faith, Naaman saying that he now knows "There is no God in all the earth, save only in Israel" (5:13), while the once blind man declares, "I believe, Lord" (John 9:38). The two Old Testament healings, mediated through the story of Asclepius (or one similar), were blended together in the oral tradition that lay behind John and were then appropriated by him to be used as the occasion for another revelation discourse ("I am the light of the world").

The greatest of Jesus' miracles in the Fourth Gospel, the resurrection of Lazarus four days after his death, has the same sort of history as the preceding one: it began as a Christian retelling of an Old Testament miracle and was then mediated through a pre-Christian myth before reaching John. Again, the Elijah-Elisha stories about the resurrection of a dead son provided the basis for this miracle of Jesus, just as they did for the resurrections of Jairus's daughter and the widow of Nain's son in the Synoptics; but the story came to John by a circuitous route. It would be difficult to trace any direct connection between the stories of Elijah and Elisha in III [I] and IV [II] Kings, on the one hand, and the story of Lazarus in John, chapter eleven, on the other, were it not that recently an earlier version of John's story was discovered, supplying evidence that suggests a line of descent.

In 1958 the American scholar Morton Smith found, at the monastery of Mar Saba in the Judaean desert a few miles from Jerusalem, an eighteenth-century copy of a letter written by Clement of Alexandria a few years before 200 A.D., in which Clement quotes a portion of a now lost Secret Gospel of Mark. Here is a part of that letter as translated by Smith:

> And they came into Bethany, and a certain woman, whose brother had died, was there. And, coming, she prostrated herself before Jesus and says to him, "Son of David, have mercy on me." But the disciples rebuked her. And Jesus, being angered, went off with her into the garden

where the tomb was, and straightway a great cry was heard from the tomb. And going near, Jesus rolled away the stone from the door of the tomb. And straightway, going in where the youth was, he stretched forth his hand and raised him seizing his hand.[7]

This is a miracle story of the synoptic type, based, like the narratives of the raising of Jairus's daughter and the widow of Nain's son, on the stories of Elijah's and Elisha's raising of dead sons. Just as the dead man's sister in the Secret Gospel approaches Jesus and prostrates herself before him to ask for help, so the Shunnamite woman whose son has died approaches Elisha and falls at his feet (IV [II] Kings 4:27). In the Secret Gospel, when the woman bows before Jesus, his disciples try to rebuke her for her precipitous act, just as in Kings, when the woman prostrates herself before Elisha, his disciple Giezi tries to thrust her away (IV [II] Kings 4:27). In both stories the prophet grows angry or speaks harshly to those attempting to stop the woman: Jesus being "angered"; Elisha saying to Giezi, "Leave her alone" (IV [II] Kings 4:27). In both, the prophet approaches the deceased, makes appropriate movements, and the dead arise. Elijah's resurrection of the widow of Sarepta's son in I Kings seems also to have influenced the story in the Secret Gospel of Mark: on the dead son's awakening, he "cried out" (III [I] Kings 17:22), just as the dead man in the Secret Gospel "gave a great cry."

But of course the most striking aspect of the story in the Secret Gospel is not its synoptic parallels; as Smith puts it, "As soon as I read the manuscript I saw that the resurrection story in it was a variant of the story of Lazarus." Smith concludes that the Secret Gospel resurrection and the story of Lazarus's resurrection both stem from some "common source which both [Secret] Mark and John used."[8] In other words, the Secret Mark source predates the Fourth Gospel and is similar to the one used by John. But obviously the story in John has either grown considerably before it reached the author of the Fourth Gospel, or he himself made major changes: there are two sisters in John, for example, and the dead man gains a name. The differences, I suggest, stem from the story's having been first mediated through a pre-Christian myth before reaching John, for these aspects of the story of Jesus' raising of Lazarus are borrowed from the Egyptian myth of the resurrection of Osiris by Horus. The earliest written form of this myth stands

> inscribed upon the walls of the chambers and passages in the pyramids of kings of the Vth and VIth dynasties at Sakkhara, and hence [is] known as the 'pyramid texts,' . . . Sections of it are found inscribed upon tombs, sarcophagi, coffins, stelae and papyri of the XIth dynasty to about A.D. 200. . . . The story of Osiris is nowhere found in a connected form in Egyptian literature, but everywhere, and in texts of all periods, the life, sufferings, death, and resurrection of Osiris are accepted as facts universally admitted.[9]

Of course the most famous narrative of Osiris is to be found in Plutarch, but the author of the Fourth Gospel seems not to have been aware of this version; his story is much closer to the mythology of the pyramid texts. Though a span of some three thousand years separates those texts from the writing of the Fourth Gospel, we can nonetheless trace the lines of connection between them; as Wallis Budge notes:

> The chief features of the Egyptian religion remained unchanged from the Vth and VIth dynasties down to the period when the Egyptians embraced Christianity, after the preaching of St. Mark the Apostle in Alexandria, A.D. 69, so firmly had the early beliefs taken possession of the Egyptian mind; and the Christians in Egypt, or Copts as they are commonly called, seem never to have succeeded in divesting themselves of the superstitious and weird mythological conceptions which they inherited.[10]

Budge continues that the "texts which have reference to the burial of the dead and to the new life in the world beyond the grave" are known "to have been in use among the Egyptians from about B.C. 4500 to the early centuries of the Christian era." Using these texts we can begin to solve one of the most fascinating questions of Johannine study and reveal, as well, the previously unrecognized source of the story of Lazarus's resurrection.

The fascinating question is why the author of the Fourth Gospel placed the resurrection of Lazarus, a story not found in the Synoptics, in Bethany. This village near Jerusalem is not known elsewhere in the Gospels as the site of a miracle; indeed, it is not even connected with Mary and Martha when they are mentioned in Luke, who merely writes that they live in "a village" (10:38). Luke mentions no brother, nor does he use the name Lazarus in connection with the two sisters. How did the author of the Fourth Gospel make the connection? I think he combined, with a faulty memory, his knowledge of the Gospels of Luke and Mark.[11] He remembered from Mark that it was "at Bethany, in the house of Simon the leper," that a certain unnamed woman had anointed Jesus with oil of nard (14:3). This was enough to move John to open his story of Lazarus thus:

> There was a man named Lazarus who had fallen ill. His home was at Bethany, the village of Mary and her sister Martha. (This Mary, whose brother Lazarus had fallen ill, was the woman who anointed the Lord with ointment and wiped his feet with her hair.) (John 11:1-2)

The woman in Bethany did not wipe Jesus' feet with her hair; rather she took a bottle of oil of nard, "broke it open and poured the oil over his head" (Mark 14:3). John has misremembered his sources, confusing this story with one in Luke, set at Nain, about another unnamed woman:

> A woman who had been living an immoral life in the town had learned that Jesus was at table in the Pharisee's house and had brought oil of myrrh in a small flask. She took her place behind him, by his feet, weeping. His feet were wetted with her tears, and she wiped them with her hair, kissing them and anointing them with the myrrh. (Luke 7:37-38)

John has blended the two stories together: the woman at Bethany
who anoints Jesus' head (but who is not described as a sinner)
becomes the sinner at Nain (though remaining at Bethany) who
wipes his feet with her hair. But neither woman is named. Mary
and Martha come from yet another story, in Luke 10:38-39, and
they live in an unnamed village:

> Jesus came to a village where a woman named Martha made him welcome
> in her home. She had a sister, Mary, who seated herself at the Lord's
> feet and stayed there listening to his words.

Thus, the Mary who sat at Jesus' feet becomes the woman who
anointed Jesus' feet, who was already misidentified with the woman
at Bethany who anointed his head. Lazarus comes, of course, from
another story in Luke, Jesus' parable of Dives and Lazarus (16:19-
31), neither of whom is related to Mary or Martha, or to Bethany.

What prompted John to put them all together as the characters
and setting of his climactic miracle story?

A Lazarus who dies, two sisters, and the village of Bethany—
all unrelated, all to be joined together in the writer's mind; there
must have been a catalyst. The answer is to be found not in the
Gospels, but in the Egyptian myth of Osiris. In the Egyptian myth,
Osiris, who dies, has two sisters, Isis and Nephthys. Osiris lies
dead at Annu, the Egyptian necropolis, known in Greek as
Heliopolis and in the Old Testament as Beth-shemesh (Jer. 43:13)—
"City of the Sun" and "House of the Sun," respectively. This
necropolis had a variety of formulaic names in Egypt: "the mansion
of the Prince in Ōn,"[12] "the House of the Aged Prince who dwelleth
in An,"[13] the "great house of Anu."[14] Just as Heliopolis was readily
semitized as Beth-shemesh, the House of Anu is readily semitized
as Beth-anu. Likewise "Lazarus" (the Greek form of the Hebrew
name "Eleazar") readily associates itself with the name of the god
Osiris (semitized as El-Osiris). Some of John's story begins to
emerge.

According to Wallis Budge, the "body of the Aged One, a name of Osiris, reposed in Annu."[15] Lazarus lies in his tomb at Bethany. The dead one is bewailed by his sisters. According to Utterance 670 of the pyramid texts, "they come to Osiris the King at the sound of the weeping of Isis, at the cry of Nephthys, at the wailing of these two spirits."[16] At Bethany, Jesus saw "Mary weeping and the Jews her companions weeping" (John 11:33). Of the dead god in Annu it is said: "O Osiris the King, you have gone, but you will return; you have slept, [but you will awake]; you have died, but you will live" (Utterance 670; square brackets are the translator's). On learning of the death of Lazarus, Jesus says, "Our friend Lazarus has fallen asleep, but I shall go and wake him" (John 11:11). Jesus approaches the tomb and says "Take away the stone" (John 11:39). To Osiris it is said, "The tomb is opened for you, the doors of the tomb-chamber are thrown open for you" (Utterance 665A). Objecting to Jesus' demand, Martha says, "Sir, by now there will be a stench; he has been there four days" (John 11:39). After Osiris is resurrected, we are told in Utterance 670, "Osiris speaks to Horus, for he has removed the evil [which was on the King] on his fourth day." Moreover, according to Utterance 412, Osiris is told, as he lies dead in the House of Annu, "O flesh of the king, do not decay, do not rot, do not smell unpleasant." The dead one in Annu/Bethany is then told to arise: "I am Horus, O Osiris the King, I will not let you suffer. Go forth, wake up" (Utterance 620): "Then he raised his voice in a great cry: 'Lazarus, come forth'" (John 11:43). The wrappings of the dead must be removed: "O King, live, for you are not dead. Horus will come to you that he may cut your cords and throw off your bonds; Horus has removed your hindrance" (Utterance 703): "The dead man came out, his hands and feet swathed in linen bands, his face wrapped in a cloth. Jesus said, 'Loose him; let him go'" (John 11:44).

The remaining question is, of course, how and in what form did the Osiris myth reach John: was it already in the form of a story about Jesus? If we are inclined to agree with Canon Streeter that "John could not, consistently with his purpose, have recorded as history any incident which he did not himself believe to have actually happened,"[17] then we might be moved to accept the theory, propounded by Bultmann and others, that John used as a literary source a "Book of Signs," which already contained the story of Lazarus, or at least the story of the resurrection of an anonymous figure with two sisters, whom John himself connected with Lazarus, who had two sisters, who lived, John surmised, based on a confused memory of passages in Mark and Luke, at Bethany—for was not Osiris raised at Beth-Annu?

This, the greatest of the "signs," brought about Jesus' death, says John, evoking not faith but opposition from the chief priests and Pharisees:

> This man is performing many signs. If we leave him alone like this the whole populace will believe in him. Then the Romans will come and sweep away our temple and our nation. (John 11:47–48)

Thus, the final sign in the Fourth Gospel brings about what is for John the great historical irony: even though Jesus was killed, the Romans still swept away the temple and the nation.

VI

THE PASSION NARRATIVES

A great obstacle to the early success of Christianity was what Paul called the stumbling-block of the cross (I Cor. 1:23). Jesus seemed not the victorious Messiah but an executed traitor—in Jewish eyes, one accursed by God (Deut. 21:23). Unless the cross could be seen as the ultimate triumph, or the pathway to it, rather than as the despairing tragedy it appeared to be, the faith of the Christians seemed vain. But this revision of perspective is just what happened, and according to Luke, it occurred between Good Friday and Pentecost, about seven weeks time. From "My God, my God, why hast thou forsaken me?" (Mark 15:34) and "They said nothing to anybody, for they were afraid" (Mark 16:8), to Peter's supreme confidence at Pentecost is a great development:

> Men of Israel, listen to me: I speak of Jesus of Nazareth, a man singled out by God and made known to you through miracles, portents, and signs, which God worked among you through him, as you well know.

When he had been given up to you, by the deliberate will and plan
of God, you used heathen men to crucify and kill him. But God raised
him to life again, setting him free from the pangs of death, because
it could not be that death should keep him in its grip. (Acts 2:22-
24)

Since Luke himself composed many of the speeches in Acts, we
cannot be certain that Peter would have expressed himself this
way so soon after the crucifixion; but it is nonetheless clear that
the early Christians did feel such confidence in the meaning and
outcome of the passion. Jesus' death was understood in the light
of the resurrection experiences; without Easter, the cross might
have remained a meaningless tragedy, but with Easter, it became
the "deliberate will and plan of God." Thus, with all confidence,
Jesus could be made to say, as he was being arrested, "Let the
scriptures be fulfilled" (Mark 14:49). What those scriptures were,
and how they were taken to be divine predictions of the passion,
and thus major sources of "information" about it, will be the subject
of this chapter.

The Gospel story of the passion begins with Mark, who possessed, in either written or oral form or in a combination of the
two, a circumstantial account of the last days of Jesus' life, beginning
with the triumphal entry into Jerusalem. Mark seems not to have
been aware that the episodes of the passion story were structured
by a series of Old Testament verses, from such books as Zechariah,
Isaiah, and the Psalms, and were for the most part carefully constructed typological fiction, happenings "according to the Scriptures." The other evangelists, however, were much more fully aware
of the biblical basis of Mark's narrative, and often looked beyond
Mark to the Old Testament and supplemented what they used
of Mark with even more fictional enlargements from the typo-
logically interpreted passages they found in the Septuagint and
Hebrew texts.

The latter chapters of Zechariah structure much of Mark's

passion narrative, beginning with the morning of the triumphal entry. This must begin from the Mount of Olives, east of Jerusalem, as Zech. 14:4 was interpreted to mean: "On that day his feet will stand on the Mount of Olives, which is opposite Jerusalem to the east." This passage lay behind a widespread Jewish belief that the Mount of Olives would see the coming of the Messiah (see, e.g., Josephus, *Jewish War,* II, 13, 5; *Antiquities,* XX, 8, 6). Thus, Mark's narrative has it that on the morning of the triumphal entry, "They were now approaching Jerusalem, and when they reached Bethphage and Bethany, at the Mount of Olives, he sent two of his disciples . . ." (11:1). Mark writes on the basis of a vague knowledge of Judaean geography, not knowing that one approaching Jerusalem from the east on the road from Jericho would reach first Bethany and then Bethphage, not the reverse order he indicates. However, the important location is the Mount of Olives; typology, not history, is at work here. The typological fiction continues on the basis of Zech. 9:9 LXX:

> Rejoice greatly, O daughter of Sion; proclaim it aloud, O daughter of Jerusalem; behold, the king is coming to thee, just, and a Saviour [*sōzōn,* "saving"]; he is meek and riding on an ass, and a young foal [*pōlon neon,* a "new (unridden) foal"].

It is only with this passage that we can understand why Mark has Jesus specify that his disciples obtain a "colt [*pōlon*] which no one has yet ridden" (Mark 11:2). Mark ignores the danger and unlikelihood of riding on an unbroken, untrained animal, assuming its miraculous tractability; typology rather than history is operative here. Even more strikingly is this the case with Matthew's treatment of Mark's narrative. Matthew draws upon another source that has combined Isa. 62:11 and Zech. 9:9:

This was to fulfil the prophecy which says: "Tell the daughters of Zion,
'Here is your king, who comes to you in gentleness, riding on an ass,
riding on the foal of a beast of burden.'" (Matt. 21:4-5)

Matthew's words agree more closely with the Hebrew text of
Zechariah than with the Septuagint, but his understanding of the
passage follows the Greek version, implying two animals: "riding
on an ass, and a young foal." Matthew wants so much for Jesus
to fulfill Zech. 9:9 (as the evangelist understands the verse) that
he invents a second donkey:

"You will at once find a donkey tethered with her foal beside her; untie
them, and bring them to me. . . . the disciples went and did as Jesus
had directed, and brought the donkey and her foal; they laid their cloaks
on them and Jesus mounted." (Matt. 21:2, 6–7)

Interestingly, the Fourth Gospel's typically careless treatment
of Old Testament citations saves it from excessive invention in
this case, since John quotes or paraphrases a garbled version of
Zechariah, mentioning only half of the parallelism; he also eliminates
the disciples' role:

Jesus found a donkey and mounted it, in accordance with the text
of Scripture: "Fear no more, daughter of Zion; see, your king is coming,
mounted on an ass's colt." (John 12:14-15)

Mark's narrative continues with another piece of typological
fiction, the joyous cry of those who witness the triumphal entry:
"Hosanna! Blessings on him who comes in the name of the Lord"
(*Eulogēmenos ho erchomenos en onomati Kuriou*)—11:9. This has
come directly quoted from the Septuagint: "Blessed is he that comes
in the name of the Lord" (*Eulogēmenos ho erchomenos en onomati
Kuriou*"—Ps. 117:25 LXX). Indeed, the closing of Mark's joyous
welcome: "Hosanna in the highest" (*Hosanna en tois hupistois*)
also quotes Ps. 148:1 LXX: "Praise him in the highest" (*ainete*

auton en tois hupistois). In both verses, Mark has imported "Hosanna" from the Hebrew or Aramaic text of Ps. 118 (117 LXX):25.

Mark's passion story continues with his account of the Last Supper, where he has consciously constructed the introduction of his narrative as a parallel to the introduction of the triumphal entry; the miraculous provision of the upper room for the meal is like the miraculous provision of the donkey:

> Now on the first day of unleavened bread, when the Passover lambs were being slaughtered, his disciples said to him, "Where would you like us to go and prepare your Passover supper?" So he sent out two of his disciples with these instructions: "Go into the city, and a man will meet you carrying a jar of water. Follow him, and when he enters a house give this message to the householder: 'The Master says, "Where is the room reserved for me to eat the Passover with my disciples?"' He will show you a large room upstairs, set out in readinesss." (Mark 14:12-15)

As Vernon K. Robbins has shown, "The common features emerge when the scenes are placed in parallel columns:

11:1-6	14:13-16
1: *he sent two of his disciples*	13: *he sent two of his disciples*
2: *and he said to them*	*and said to them,*
and . . . you will find	*and . . . will meet you . . .*
3: *Say, "The Lord . . .*	14: *Say . . ., "The*
4: *And they went away,*	16: *And they went out . . .*
and they found . . .	*and found*
6: as Jesus had said,	*as he had told them;*
and	*and. . ."*[1]

We see Mark's own fictive imagination and literary style at work in his introduction to the Last Supper. The fiction about Judas that follows, however, probably comes from Mark's source, as it is based on an unrecognized allusion that is made explicit only in the Fourth Gospel. Mark has it that Jesus miraculously knew in advance that "one of you will betray me." That the knowledge is typological fiction becomes clear in the rest of the verse: "one who is eating with me" (14:18). Probably without realizing what his source has done, Mark presents Jesus alluding to Psalm 40 (41):5 LXX: "Even the man of my peace, in whom I trusted, who ate my bread, lifted up his heel against me." Mark's allusion becomes explicit, as does the rest of the fiction, in the Fourth Gospel; John has Jesus declare that "there is a text of Scripture to be fulfilled: "He who eats bread with me has turned against me" (13:18). This making explicit the implicit typological fiction continues in John's account of the Last Supper. Whereas Mark has Jesus "knowing," on the basis of the supposed prediction in Ps. 40 LXX, that "one of you [unspecified] will betray me," John presents Jesus knowing exactly who the betrayer was, with a fictional expansion of a verse in Mark: "'It is one of the Twelve,' he said, 'who is dipping into the same bowl with me'" (Mark 14:20). For John, Jesus' miraculous foreknowledge of the identity of the betrayer is another piece of evidence of his divinity: "I tell you this now, before the event, so that when it happens you may believe that I am what I am" (John 13:19). Thus, when the Beloved Disciple asks, "Lord, who is it?" Jesus replies, "'It is the man to whom I give this piece of bread when I have dipped it in the dish.' Then, after dipping it in the dish, he took it out and gave it to Judas son of Simon Iscariot" (John 13:26). So the one "who ate my bread" (Ps. 40:5 LXX) becomes revealed as Judas before the betrayal; we see the typological fiction growing before our eyes. Indeed, Septuagint Psalm 40 helped create another aspect of the Judas legend, as we see later in this chapter, for this Psalm was traditionally interpreted in Judaism as being written by David and referring to his counselor Ahithophel, who betrayed his master and then hanged himself, events taken as predictive of the fate of Judas.

It was Mark who first presented, for theological purposes, the fiction that the Last Supper was a Passover meal; Matthew

and Luke follow his lead in this, but John makes it quite clear
that, in his view, the Last Supper was not a Passover meal; rather,
it happened the night before Passover (see John 13:1; 18:28; 19:14).
It seems likely that John is right in this case and that the Paschal
significance of the Last Supper is Mark's fiction. The earliest account
of this meal is Paul's, which makes no mention of Passover and
assumes that the "Lord's supper" is a full meal eaten regularly
at Christian gatherings. Paul's account is obviously part of the
same kind of tradition that Mark drew upon and has clear Christian
liturgical significance, with no Paschal connotations at all:

> For the tradition which I handed on to you came to me from the
> Lord himself: that the Lord Jesus, on the night of his arrest, took bread
> and, after giving thanks to God, broke it and said: "This is my body,
> which is for you; do this as a memorial of me." In the same way,
> he took the cup after supper, and said: "This cup is the new covenant
> sealed by my blood. Whenever you drink it, do this as a memorial
> of me." (I Cor. 11:23-25)

Mark's version of the tradition either had no liturgical significance,
no "do this as a memorial," or Mark deliberately removed it;
moreover, the central biblical allusion in Mark's scene, one not
found in Paul's, is explicitly non-Paschal, referring to the covenant
scene at Sinai, which happened three months after the first Passover:

> During supper he took bread, and having said the blessing he broke
> it and gave it to them, with the words: "Take this; this is my body."
> Then he took a cup, and having offered thanks to God he gave it
> to them; and they all drank from it. And he said, "This is my blood,
> the blood of the covenant, shed for many." (Mark 14:22-24)

Mark's source has Jesus allude to Exodus 24:8: "This is the blood
of the covenant which the LORD has made with you." In Paul's
version the central biblical allusion is to Jeremiah 31:31: "I will
make a new covenant with Israel and Judah"—another verse with

no Paschal significance. Though Mark calls it a Passover meal, his description of what happens there, which he found in the kind of tradition Paul also used, is not a description of a Passover meal; no bitter herbs are mentioned, as is required by Numbers 9:11, and no Passover liturgy is recited; indeed, "pes 10:5 attributes to R. Gamaliel (first century A.D.) a tradition that whoever does not mention the lamb, unleavened bread, and bitter herbs at the meal has not fulfilled his passover obligation."[2] Moreover, the arrest account that Mark inherited insisted that Jesus was *not* arrested during the Passover festival: "The chief priests and the doctors of the law were trying to devise some cunning plan to seize him and put him to death. 'It must not be during the festival,' they said, 'or we should have rioting among the people'" (Mark 14:1-2). Mark inherited a tradition of the Lord's Supper that was already part of Christian liturgy and fictionally turned it into a Passover meal for his own theological purposes, which become clear in the introduction to his account in 14:12: "Now on the first day of Unleavened Bread, when the Passover lambs were being slaughtered, his disciples said to him, 'Where would you like us to go and prepare for your Passover supper?'" So even though the Cup Word, "my blood, the blood of the covenant," is not a Passover saying in Mark's narrative, Jesus' blood is for Mark nonetheless symbolically equivalent to that of the Passover lamb.

Strangely, the Fourth Gospel attributes Paschal significance to Jesus' death *without* turning the Last Supper into a Passover meal, by having John the Baptist identify Jesus as the "Lamb of God" (1:29), and depicting Jesus as dying on the afternoon *before* Passover, at the same time as the lambs were being slaughtered in Jerusalem.

We cannot, in other words, know when Jesus died—the afternoon before Passover or the afternoon after—because the accounts are theological fiction rather than the kind of history for which chronology is basic. Nor could we know, even if the Cup Word and the Bread Word were actual statements rather than theological fiction created from Old Testament passages, what Jesus actually said—whether "Take this; this is my body," or "This is my body, which is for you; do this as a memorial of me"; whether "This is my blood, the blood of the covenant," or "This cup is the new covenant sealed by my blood. Whenever you drink it, do this as a memorial of me."

The next episode after the Last Supper, the story of Jesus' agony in the garden of Gethsemane, is one of the most moving fictional creations in the New Testament. Though Mark's Gospel is the first to tell the story in written form, its origins in the Old Testament are more clearly revealed in Luke's version, whose vocabulary betrays its origins in Septuagint III Kings 19, the story of Elijah's fleeing from Ahab and Jezebel. In both stories the prophet (Elijah, Jesus) knows that the rulers (Ahab, the Jerusalem authorities) seek his arrest and death. In both, the prophet leaves behind his servant or disciples and seeks solitude under a tree (Elijah) or in a garden among olive trees (Jesus), where he prays to be delivered (take my soul; take this cup from me). In both, an angel appears to strengthen him (telling Elijah to "arise"; as Jesus tells his followers to "arise"); the prophet then goes forth to meet his fate. Only Luke's version depicts the appearance of the angel to Jesus in Gethsemane, revealing in its vocabulary a dependence on Septuagint III Kings and thus the origins of the story: "And now there appeared to him an angel [*aggelos*] from heaven bringing him strength [*enischuōn*]" (22:43-44); in Kings, an angel (*aggelos*) appears to Elijah, helping him to go forth "in strength [*en ischui*]" (III Kings 19:8 LXX).

Mark's version of the story, however, has lost this sign of its origins, revealing other biblical bases, especially for the speeches of Jesus. Mark's pericope has two main purposes: the lesser is to continue his almost obsessive theme of the inadequacy of the disciples to their task; the major purpose is to show Jesus humbling himself, in fulfilment of scripture, to the divine will, thus demonstrating his worthiness to be our Redeemer. Even beyond its

apparent origins (as revealed by Luke) in the Old Testament, the
account is obviously fictional, since there could have been no
witnesses to Jesus' agony in the garden after he left his followers;
they were all, according to the story, asleep. Jesus' emotional agony
was part of the typological fiction, as well as part of Mark's overall
sense of Jesus' supernatural foreknowledge: just as he knew that
one of his followers would betray him, so he knew that he would
be taken on this very night:

> When they reached a place called Gethsemane, he said to his disciples,
> "Sit here while I pray." And he took Peter and James and John with
> him. Horror and dismay came over him, and he said to them, "My
> soul is deeply grieved, even unto death; stop here, and stay awake."
> (Mark 14:32-34)

The main biblical models here were in Septuagint Jonah and the
Psalms. In the fourth chapter of his book, the prophet Jonah finds
himself "deeply grieved" (4:1), just as Jesus in Gethsemane is "deeply
grieved." Both pray in their distress, Jonah declaring that "I am
greatly grieved, even unto death" (*sphodra leluppēmai ego heōs
thanatou*—Jonah 4:9 LXX); Jesus praying that "My soul is greatly
grieved, even unto death" (*perilupos estin hē psychē mou heōs
thanatou*—Mark 14:34). The passage in Mark may also have been
influenced by Psalm 42:5 LXX, where the psalmist asks why "is
my soul very grieved?" (*perilupos ei hē psychē mou*).

The rest of Jonah's prayer is not a suitable model for Mark's
scene (he petulantly tells the Lord to "take my life; I should be
better dead than alive"—4:3), so the early Christian writer went
again to the Psalms, those classic religious outcries of the troubled
soul. Here we may observe the process by which Mark's fiction
grew. Underlying the story of the entire Thursday evening before
the crucifixion are a number of biblical *loci*, especially the books
of Zechariah, Jonah, and the Psalms. Mark was apparently only
minimally aware of the biblical basis of his traditions, but the other

three evangelists were, in their own ways, much more fully cognizant of the "fulfillment" of Scripture in the accounts they possessed. At the end of the Passover supper, says Mark, "After singing the Passover Hymn, they went out to the Mount of Olives" (14:26). Matthew knew that the traditional Passover Hymns were to be found in Psalms 113-118, the first two of which were sung before the meal, the last four afterward; thus the first evangelist (if not the others) would have been aware that Jesus had just finished singing the following words (aware, that is, that any Jew would have sung them, thus Jesus *must* have):

> My distress was bitter.
> In panic I cried,
>   "How faithless all men are!" . . .
> I will take in my hands the cup of salvation
> and invoke the LORD by name.
> I will pay my vows to the LORD
> in the presence of all his people.
> A precious thing in the LORD's sight
> is the death of those who die faithful to him.
>   (Ps. 116:10-15)

On these very words, therefore, Jesus would have been meditating, someone must have surmised, as he walked with his disciples toward Gethsemane. The psalmist had "predicted" the faithlessness of "all men"; thus, Jesus must have said to his disciples, "You will all fall from your faith" (Mark 14:27), and he would think of his coming suffering as a "cup." Since the psalmist had "predicted" it, Jesus must also feel distress and panic, or horror and dismay, in Mark's words, and plead, "Father . . . take this cup away from me" (Mark 14:36). But Jesus' dismay would only be momentary; the Psalm assures it:

I love the LORD, for he has heard me and listens to my prayer;
for he has given me a hearing whenever I have cried to him. . . .
Anguish and torment held me fast;
so I invoked the LORD by name,
Deliver me, O LORD, I beseech thee.

(Ps. 116:1-4)

Thus, the development of Jesus' emotions on this night of agony
in the garden follows the development of the passover hymn, Psalm
116: from fear and agony, to prayer, to resolution and determination
to take the cup: "Yet not what I will, but what thou wilt" (Mark
14:36).

After Jesus' prayer and resolution:

He came back and found them asleep; and he said to Peter, "Asleep,
Simon? Were you not able to stay awake for one hour? Stay awake,
all of you; and pray." (Mark 14:37-38)

Mark's source then turned for his account of Jesus' movements
to Jonah 1:6, where the ship's captain approaches the prophet on
the night of the great storm: "What, sound asleep?" he said. "Get
up, and call upon your god." This verse also structures the
subsequent scene in Mark, when Jesus again returns to his disciples:
"Still sleeping . . .? Arise" (Mark 14:41-42).

The principal source of the story of Jesus' arrest, beginning
with the cowardice of his disciples, is the book of Zechariah. Since
their cowardice was so humiliating afterwards, so little calculated
to heighten their stature in the eyes of the early Christians, it may
well be historical. But their weakness and blindness (had not Jesus
three times predicted this?) could at least be presented as the deliberate
will and plan of God. Thus Mark begins his account of the arrest
with a reference to Zechariah: "Jesus said, 'You will all fall from
your faith; for it stands written: "I will strike the shepherd down
and the sheep will be scattered"'" (Mark 14:26-27). Mark's source
in the tradition cites Zech. 13:7, the shepherd referring, in the

Christian interpretation, to Jesus, and the sheep being the eleven faithful disciples. What Mark apparently did not know was that the context of this verse stood as the script for his source's account of much of the arrest scene, and that the shepherd was subject to a second interpretation as the "worthless shepherd" (Zech. 11:17), who was in fact the model for Judas Iscariot. Mark's reference to Zech. 13:7 is from the Aramaic or Hebrew text rather than the Septuagint, usually a sign that Mark has inherited a traditional reference rather than having composed his own in Greek.

Zechariah, in chapter eleven, describes the worthless shepherd who will sell his flock to the slaughterers rather than succor them. He will "have no pity" for his flock, but will rather be more interested to say "I am rich" (Zech. 11:5). Just as Jesus says at the Last Supper, "Alas for that man by whom the Son of Man is betrayed" (Mark 14:4), so Zechariah says, "Alas for the worthless shepherd" (Zech. 11:17), for he says to his flock, "I will not fatten you any more. Any that are to die, let them die." He then breaks his shepherd's staffs and abandons his office. But "the dealers who were watching me knew that all this was the word of the LORD." The worthless shepherd then says to the dealers: "'If it suits you, give me my wages, otherwise keep them.' Then they weighed out my wages, thirty pieces of silver" (Zech. 11:12). The fate of this worthless shepherd, who sells his sheep for slaughter, will be terrible: "Alas for the worthless shepherd who abandons his sheep! A sword shall fall on his arm and on his right eye" (Zech. 11:17). In Mark this fate is transferred to one of those arresting Jesus, who is struck with a sword by one of Jesus' followers. In Mark's source, the worthless shepherd who sells his sheep becomes Judas Iscariot, who "went to the chief priests, to betray him to them. When they heard what he had come for, they were greatly pleased, and promised him money" (Mark 14:10-11). Mark does not name the amount of money and does not appear to recognize that Zechariah was interpreted by his source as a prophecy of Jesus' arrest. Matthew, however, did recognize that this was the case, as we can see by his treatment of Mark:

> Then Judas Iscariot, one of the Twelve, went to the chief priests to betray him to them. When they heard what he had come for, they were greatly pleased, and promised him money; and he began to look for a good opportunity to betray him. (Mark 14:10-11)

> Then one of the Twelve, the man called Judas Iscariot, went to the chief priests and said, "What will you give me to betray him to you?" They weighed him out thirty silver pieces. From that moment he began to look out for an opportunity to betray him. (Matt. 26:14-15)

Matthew read Mark, observed its transparency upon Zechariah, and changed Judas's intention to betray and the priests' promise of money into a direct question from Judas; then Matthew paraphrased Zechariah 11:12, "They weighed out my wages, thirty pieces of silver." At this point Matthew's method of composition becomes especially interesting. Mark had said nothing about the fate of Judas Iscariot after Jesus' arrest, only that the priests promised to pay him money, not even indicating whether the money was ever paid. But the Christian sense of retribution could not rest with this, and soon legends were circulating that Judas died horribly. Luke knew one of those legends:

> This Judas, be it noted, after buying a plot of land with the price of his villainy, fell forward on the ground, and burst open, so that his entrails poured out. This became known to everyone in Jerusalem, and they named the property in their own language Akeldama, which means "Blood Acre." (Acts 1:18-19)

As might be expected, early Christians, in order to find out what happened to Judas, went to their usual source, the Old Testament. As Luke has Peter say just before the story of Judas's death, "The prophecy in scripture was bound to come true, which the Holy Spirit, through the mouth of David, uttered about Judas"; Peter then cites Psalms 69 and 109 as oracles about Judas Iscariot. But before Luke has Peter quote the passages, he inserts the statement about Judas's buying the plot of land and dying. It is not found in the Psalms, but in another passage which early Christians read as a prediction about Judas; like Mark, Luke here seems ignorant of where his source sought information about the plot of land, the Book of Jeremiah: "I bought the field at Anathoth from my cousin Hanamel and weighed out the price, seventeen shekels of silver" (Jer. 32:10).

Jeremiah then takes the deeds of purchase and deposits "them in an earthenware jar" (Jer. 32:14). Though Luke does not identify Jeremiah as the source of his information about Judas's purchase of a field, we fortunately know with certainty that Jeremiah is the book to which early Christians went for such information, because Matthew, in his version of the story, tells us so. Still, he gets his facts wrong in a very revealing way:

> When Judas the traitor saw that Jesus had been condemned, he was seized with remorse, and returned the thirty silver pieces to the chief priests and elders. "I have sinned," he said; "I have brought an innocent man to his death." But they said, "What is that to us? See to that yourself." So he threw the money down in the temple and left them, and went and hanged himself. Taking up the money, the chief priests argued: "This cannot be put into the temple fund; it is blood-money." So after conferring they used it to buy the Potter's Field, as a burial-place for foreigners. This explains the name "Blood Acre," by which that field has been known ever since; and in this way fulfilment was given to the prophetic utterance of Jeremiah: "They took the thirty silver pieces, the price set on a man's head (for that was his price among the Israelites), and gave the money for the potter's field, as the Lord directed me." (Matt. 27:3-10)

As it happens, the passage Matthew quotes is not from Jeremiah at all, but is a muddled paraphrase of Zechariah 11:12-13:

> I said to them, "If it suits you, give me my wages, otherwise keep them." Then they weighed out my wages, thirty pieces of silver. The LORD said to me, "Throw it into the treasury" [here the Hebrew literally

reads "Throw it to the potter"]. I took the thirty pieces of silver—
that noble sum at which I was valued and rejected by them!—and threw
them into the house of the LORD, into the treasury [lit.: "to the potter"].

That Matthew thinks the passage he is quoting comes from Jeremiah
shows that he has departed from his usual practice—especially
when using Mark—of checking the accuracy of his source's Old
Testament reference. Matthew's source has blended Jeremiah's
buying of a field and placing the deed in a pot with Zechariah's
casting of thirty pieces of silver into the treasury (or to the potter),
to create the fiction about Judas's casting *his* thirty pieces of silver
down in the temple and the purchase of the Potter's Field. The
story of Judas's actions after the betrayal is one of the most revealing
examples of the early Christians' fictional and imaginative use of
the Old Testament as a book about Jesus. Here, two different
legends have grown out of a combination of Jeremiah and
Zechariah, one in which Judas bought Blood Acre, the other in
which the priests bought it.

That there were two such legends also accounts for the two
different stories about Judas's death: he hangs himself in Matthew
and bursts open in Acts. Both versions of the death are based
on oracular readings of the Old Testament. Since Luke shows Peter
going to Psalms 69 and 109 for predictions about Judas, it is possible
that Luke's legend about Judas's bursting open comes from a
muddled reading of Psalm 137:9: "Happy is he who shall seize
your children and dash them against the rock." We need not
speculate about the biblical source of Matthew's legend, for the
Old Testament has a close parallel about a traitor who hangs himself—Ahithophel, who betrayed David by going over to Absalom's
rebellion, only to find his counsel ignored:

When Ahithophel saw that his advice had not been taken he saddled
his ass, went straight home to his city, gave his last instructions to
his household, and hanged himself. (II Sam. 17:23)

Matthew uses the same Greek word for "he hanged himself" (*apēg-xato*—27:5) as does the Septuagint.

Though Jesus must certainly have been captured by the authorities before he was killed, the arrest scene in Mark is a fictional episode based largely on Old Testament passages read as predictions—"Let the scriptures be fulfilled," Jesus says as he is taken—and the scenes in Matthew, Luke, and John are variations on Mark's basic fiction.

As some scholars have argued, the arrest scene seems contrived and unnecessary. Jesus and his movements were well known to the authorities; there was no need to resort to the "slippery aid of hired traitors"[3] in order to capture him. "Day after day I was within your reach as I taught in the temple," Jesus reminds them at his arrest (Mark 14:49); it was hardly necessary to betray with a kiss one already so well known: that act is fulfilled prophecy. The early Christians remembered that "the kisses of an enemy are perfidious" (Prov. 27:6); they also remembered the story in II Sam. 20:9-10, when Joab "came forward, concealing his treachery, and said to Amasa, 'I hope you are well, my brother,' and with his right hand he grasped Amasa's beard to kiss him. Amasa was not on his guard against the sword in Joab's hand. Joab struck him with it in the belly." We know that this passage became one of the bases of the story of Judas, because it is again echoed in Luke's version of the traitor's death. For when Joab stabbed Amasa in the belly, we learn from the Septuagint, Luke's source, that "his bowels poured out [*exechuthē*] upon the ground" (II Kings [II Sam.] 20:10 LXX), just as when Judas died, "he burst open, so that his entrails poured out [*exechuthē*]" (Acts 1:18). And as we have seen, the same Old Testament book supplied Matthew's version of the death of the traitor, suicide by hanging.

The Trial

The story of Jesus' trial begins with Mark, who possessed conflicting traditions which he tried to reconcile. The other evangelists build upon Mark, largely from the Old Testament.

Mark's account of the trial must be speculative, since there were no followers of Jesus present to report on it later: "the disciples all deserted him and ran away" at his arrest (Mark 14:50). Early Christians, in composing an account of the trial, followed the usual method of gathering information about Jesus in the absence of real evidence: they went to the Old Testament.

The scene before the Sanhedrin begins with a combination of passages from Daniel and the Psalms. The effort to find evidence against Jesus comes first of all from the Septuagint version of Daniel: "Then the governors and satraps sought [*ezētoun*] to find [*heurein*] occasion against Daniel; but they found against him [*ouch heuron*] no occasion" (Dan. 6:4 LXX). This is echoed in Mark: "The chief priests and the whole Council sought [*ezētoun*] testimony against Jesus in order to kill him, but they found none" [*ouch heuriskon*] (Mark 14:55). Subsequent verses in Mark come from either the Twenty-seventh or Thirty-fifth Psalm:

"Some having stood up [*anastantes*] gave false evidence [*epseudomarturoun*] against him" (Mark 14:57)

"Unjust witnesses standing up [*anastantes martures adikoi*] asked [*epērōtōn*] me" (Ps. 34[35]:11 LXX)

"The high priest, standing up, [*anastas*] in the midst, asked [*epērōtēse*] Jesus" (Mark 14:60)

"Many gave false evidence against him, but their testimonies were not consistent" (Mark 14:56)

"Unjust witnesses [*martures adikoi*] have stood up [*epanestēsan*] against me, and injustice has lied [*epseusato*] within herself" (Ps. 26[27]:12 LXX)

There is confusion in the tradition about the charge against Jesus from the false witnesses:

> Some stood up and gave false evidence against him to this effect: "We
> heard him say, 'I will pull down this temple, made with human hands,
> and in three days I will build another, not made with hands.'" But
> even on this point their evidence did not agree. (Mark 14:57-59)

But what to Mark is false evidence is genuine to John, who has
Jesus declare, "Destroy this temple, . . . and in three days I will
raise it again." Jesus' hearers think he means the Jerusalem temple,
but John asserts: "The temple he was speaking of was his body"
(John 2:19, 21). Perhaps Mark possessed the saying and used it
on his own authority as the charge against Jesus.

Because the famous Suffering Servant passage in Isa. 53 became
so important to early Christian understanding of the passion, and
because 53:7 says, "He did not open his mouth," there early arose
a tradition of Jesus' silence before the Sanhedrin: "He kept silence;
he made no reply" (Mark 14:61). But Mark also possessed a legend
that Jesus did speak at his trial, declaring, in answer to the question,
"Are you the Messiah?" an unequivocal "I am" (*ego eimi*—Mark
14:62). Matthew was apparently troubled by the conflict, so he
introduced into Mark's second question from the High Priest a
new element. Mark simply has the priest ask, "Are you the Messiah,
the Son of the Blessed One?"—Mark 14:61. Matthew, however,
adds a phrase: "By the living God I charge [*exorkizo*] you to tell
us: Are you the Messiah, the Son of God?"—Matt. 26:63. Appearing
to be casting about for a way to make sense out of Mark's having
it both ways—that Jesus both spoke and did not speak before
the Sanhedrin—Matthew introduced into the scene a requirement
from Leviticus 5:1: "If a person hears a solumn adjuration [*horkismu*
LXX] to give evidence as a witness to something he has seen or
heard and does not declare what he knows, he commits a sin
and must accept responsibility." By echoing Leviticus in his addition
to Mark's version of the High Priest's question, Matthew thus
accounts for the fact that Jesus answers in spite of the prophecy
in Isa. 53 that he will not open his mouth. Interestingly, too, Matthew

drops half of Mark's statement about Jesus' lack of response to
the High Priest's first question; in Mark 14:61 we find, "But he
kept silence; he made no reply," whereas in Matthew 26:53 we
find only, "But Jesus kept silence." Matthew drops "he made no
reply" in order to help make sense of the fact that Jesus replies
to the next question. Matthew 26:64 nevertheless preserves the non-
answer prophesied in Isaiah by turning Mark's "I am" into the
ambiguous "The words are yours" (lit.: you have said).

We find another typical example of Matthew's literary skill
in his treatment of the "blasphemy" aspect of the trial. In Mark,
where both Jesus and the High Priest through circumlocution take
great care to avoid direct use of the word "God", the scene goes
like this:

> Again the High Priest questioned him: "Are you the Messiah, the Son
> of the Blessed One?" Jesus said, "I am; and you will see the Son of
> Man seated at the right hand of the Power [*tēs dunameōs*] and coming
> with the clouds of heaven." Then the High Priest tore his robes and
> said, "Need we call further witnesses? You have heard the blasphemy."
> (Mark 14:62-64)

Matthew, however, wittily turns the High Priest himself into the
blasphemer, changing Mark so that the High Priest twice uses
"God" in his question: "By the living God I charge you to tell
us: Are you the Messiah the Son of God?" (Matt. 26:63)

For what happened to Jesus at this point, Mark's source had
gone to Isaiah 50:6 in the Septuagint: "I gave my back to scourges,
and my cheeks to blows [*hrapismata*]; and I turned not away my
face from the shame of spitting [*emptusmatōn*]," and follows it
closely: "Some began to spit [*emptuein*] on him, blindfolded him,
and struck him [*hrapismasin*]" (Mark 14:65).

The Crucifixion

That Jesus was crucified by the Romans—the usual method of executing rebels—is the historical basis of the Gospel accounts of Jesus' death (Mark 15, Matt. 27, Luke 23, John 19); the accounts are nevertheless fiction, composed for theological purposes.

> Then they took him out to crucify him. A man called Simon, from Cyrene, the father of Alexander and Rufus, was passing by on his way in from the country, and they pressed him into service to carry his cross. They brought him to the place called Golgotha, which means "Place of a Skull." (Mark 15:21-22)

This seems straightforward enough, and even vouchsafes that the sons of one actually present at the crucifixion are known to the writer and his community, thus ensuring that Mark's account of the event is historically correct. The Fourth Gospel likewise declares firmly that its account of events at the crucifixion is "vouched for by an eyewitness, whose evidence is to be trusted" (John 19:35); yet, according to John, "Jesus was now taken in charge and, carrying his own cross, went out to the Place of the Skull, as it is called (or, in the Jews' language, 'Golgotha')" (John 19:17). We can never decide which version is "correct," nor know for certain whether Jesus carried his own cross, for the two accounts exist not for historical reasons, but from theological or apologetic need.

Look closely at the Greek of Mark's account of Simon of Cyrene: they pressed him into service "to carry his cross" (*hina arē ton stauron autou*—Mark 15:21); compare it with Jesus' words about the job of a Christian disciple: "Whoever wishes to follow me, let him deny himself, let him bear his cross (*aratō ton stauron autou*), and let him follow me" (Mark 8:34). Mark has used the same words; Simon is literally following Jesus with the cross in a symbolic enactment of what it means to be a Christian. Mark 15:21 is an enacted parable of the Christian life, composed perhaps by Mark himself. Why the name Simon? Go back to Mark's source for the line "bear the cross" in chapter 8; Jesus has just delivered the first passion prediction ("the Son of Man had to undergo great suffering, and . . . to be put to death"):

> At this Peter took him by the arm and began to rebuke him. But Jesus turned around, and, looking at his disciples, rebuked Peter. "Away with you, Satan," he said, "you think as men think, not as God thinks." (Mark 8:33)

Then Jesus delivers his saying about taking up one's cross. Mark simply reverses the scene in chapter 15, where a Simon does take up the cross instead of rebuking Jesus when he speaks of his own way to the cross. Indeed, Mark amasses irony here: for when in chapter 8 Jesus says, "Whoever wishes to follow me, let him deny himself" (*aparnēsasthō*), Mark has Jesus use the same word to Simon Peter in chapter 15: "Thrice you will deny me" (*aparnēsē*). Simon of Cyrene is given as the Christian model, not Simon Peter, in keeping with Mark's almost obsessive theme of the inadequacy of the original circle of disciples (on which, see especially S. G. F. Brandon, *The Fall of Jerusalem and the Christian Church*).

If, as many hold, the author of the Fourth Gospel knew Mark's work, why did he assert so strongly, contradicting Mark, that Jesus carried his own cross? Again the answer is a matter of theology rather than history. The Fourth Gospel was written, in part, as an attack upon Gnostic Christianity, which held that the Son of God was not really crucified; some Gnostics in fact held that Simon of Cyrene not only carried the cross, but was himself killed upon it. John dealt with that argument simply by eliminating Simon altogether. Moreover, John has an entirely different picture of Jesus' condition at the crucifixion. In the Synoptics, the implication is that Jesus is too weak, following his scourging and beating, to carry his own cross; but for John, Jesus is entirely triumphant throughout the passion. John presents no cry of dereliction from the cross ("My God, my God, why hast thou forsaken me?") but instead insists that the dying words were a cry of triumph: "It is accomplished!" (19:30). Such a figure was quite capable of carrying a cross.

Mark's next verse again seems straightforward historical narrative: "He was offered drugged wine, but he would not take it" (15:23). Mark had written, in the preceding chapter, Jesus' words at the Last Supper: "Never again shall I drink from the fruit of the vine until I drink it new in the kingdom of God" (14:25)— so Jesus *must* have refused wine, even though Mark describes the offer as an act of mercy, a painkiller (myrrhed wine). Matthew later corrects Mark on the basis of what he regards as a more "accurate" account, the Sixty-ninth Psalm in the Septuagint: "They gave [*edōkan*] me also gall [*cholēn*] for my food, and made me drink vinegar [*oxos*]" (Ps. 69 [70]:21). Thus Matthew: "They gave [*edōkan*] him wine mixed with gall [*cholēs*], but having tasted it he refused to drink" (27:34). Matthew changes the Roman soldiers' act of mercy (drugged wine) to an act of cruel mockery (undrinkably bitter wine) by reading through Mark to a previously unrecognized "prediction" in the Old Testament. Fascinatingly, Luke does the same thing, but on the basis of the *other* part of Ps. 69:21 LXX, "They . . . made me drink vinegar [*oxos*]": "The soldiers joined in the mockery and came forward offering him their sour wine [*oxos*]" (23:26). "Knowing" on the basis of the Psalm, as did Matthew, that the offer of wine was mockery, Luke also drops Mark's statement that the soldiers' wine was drugged with myrrh.

John adds another symbolic fiction based on the Old Testament. Knowing from his source (probably Mark) that the dying Jesus was offered vinegar (*oxos*) and that this act was in fulfilment of scripture, he also seems to have been aware that David (prophetically) declared, "Sprinkle me with hyssop" (Ps. 51:7); John proceeds to blend the two "prophetic" Psalms together as sources for a key detail at the crucifixion:

> After that, Jesus, aware that all had now come to its appointed end,
> said in fulfilment of Scripture, "I thirst." A jar stood there full of sour
> wine [oxous]; so they soaked a sponge with the wine, fixed it on hyssop,
> and held it to his lips. (John 19:28-29)

John's source for the event, though not the speech "I thirst," is
Mark: when Jesus cries, "Why hast thou forsaken me?" the "bystanders, on hearing this, said, 'Hark, he is calling Elijah'" (for
Mark had written Jesus' cry in Aramaic, "*Eli, Eli* [My God, my
God]." "A man ran and soaked a sponge in sour wine and held
it to his lips on the end of a cane" (Mark 15:34-36). Because he
will not allow that terrible cry of dereliction from the cross, John
has had to invent another speech that will bring the wine on the
sponge, and he too goes to Septuagint Psalm 69:21: "They . . .
made me drink vinegar [oxos] for my thirst," changing the last
words into direct discourse (*dipsan*, "thirst," to *Dipsō*, "I thirst").
But why change "sponge on the end of a cane [kalamō]" to a
"sponge on hyssop [hussōpō]?" I would suggest that the marjoram
or hyssop comes not only from the Psalms but also is a way for
John to introduce more Paschal symbolism into the crucifixion.
Remember that the first phrase uttered about Jesus in the Fourth
Gospel is the Baptist's "Behold the lamb of God" (1:29), and that
John presents Jesus dying even as the Passover lambs were being
slaughtered in Jerusalem. According to Exodus, hyssop (marjoram)
was to be used for sprinkling the blood of the Paschal lamb on
the doorposts and lintels of Hebrew homes (12:21); thus, the
touching of Jesus with hyssop becomes the symbolic reenactment
of the Passover ritual upon his own person.

   Mark continues his account of the Crucifixion:

> Then they fastened him to the cross. They divided [*diamerizontai*] his
> clothes [*himatia*] among them, casting lots [*ballontes klēron*] to decide
> what each should have. (15:24)

He is still apparently unaware of its being structured by the Twenty-second Psalm:

> They parted my garments [*Diemerisanto ta himatia mou*] among themselves, and cast lots [*ebalon klēron*] for my raiment. (Ps. 21 [22]:18 LXX)

Matthew and Luke follow Mark closely and without elaboration. John, however, creating symbolism out of the episode, blends Mark's scene with an allusion to the sacerdotal garment of the high priest, a role Jesus, offering himself as the Passover lamb, had symbolically assumed for the fourth evangelist:

> The soldiers, having crucified Jesus, took possession of his clothes [*himatia*], and divided them into four parts, one for each soldier, leaving out the tunic [*chitōna*]. The tunic was seamless, woven in one piece throughout; so they said to one another, "We must not tear this; let us toss for it"; and then the text of Scripture came true: "They shared my garments [*himatia*] among them, and cast lots for my clothing [*himatismon*]."

Only John among the four quotes LXX Ps. 21:18 in its entirety, reading the simple parallelism of the verse as two separate actions and introducing Jesus' tunic (*chitōna*) into the episode; he does this in order to echo Leviticus 16:4, which declares that the high priest, when entering the Most Holy, shall "put on the consecrated linen tunic [*chitōna*—LXX]." Moreover, Jewish practice called for this tunic to be seamless, as we know from Josephus's *Antiquities* and as John would have known: "It cannot be torn" (Ex. 28:32).

Mark continues: "The hour of the crucifixion was nine in the morning" (the third hour, Roman time—Mark 15:25); John, however, tells us that "It was the eve of Passover, about noon," when Pilate "handed Jesus over to be crucified." Thus, we cannot know the hour of the crucifixion. Nor, in fact, did the evangelists know; their times were fictional creations, parts of a theological framework.

For John, Jesus must die even as the Paschal lambs are being slaughtered, and die for the same reason. For Mark (and the other Synoptics after him), Jesus must suffer for six hours, from 9 A.M. (Mark 15:25) until 3 P.M. (Mark 15:33), so that on the seventh or sabbath hour he could complete his task, and rest, as did his Father after the six days of creation. Something analogous is also true of the day of Jesus' death. Remember that John had written, "It was the eve of Passover" when Jesus was crucified; the Synoptics, on the other hand, make perfectly clear that the Last Supper was a Passover supper. We therefore cannot know whether Jesus died on the afternoon before the Passover meal or on the afternoon following it. The real point in all four Gospels is that the crucifixion is the ultimate Passover sacrifice, not the actual time or day of the event, both of which are fictional. Northrop Frye's principle applies: "If anything historically true is in the Bible, it is there not because it is historically true but for different reasons. The reasons presumably have something to do with spiritual profundity or significance."[4]

Mark continues:

> The passers-by [*paraporeuomenoi*] hurled abuse at him: "Aha!" they cried, wagging their heads, "you would pull the temple down, would you, and build it in three days? Come down from the cross and save yourself."(Mark 15:29–32)

The opening of this verse came to Mark from Christian tradition; it is based upon the Twenty-second Psalm and perhaps influenced by Lamentations 2:15 in the Septuagint: "All who see me jeer at me, make mouths at me and wag their heads" (Ps. 22:7). A passage in Lamentations seems also to relate to this Psalm and to Mark's account: "All that go by the way [*paraporeuomenoi*] have clapped their hands at thee, they have hissed and shaken their head" (Lam. 2:15 LXX).

Mark appears not to have realized the basis of the verse in

the Septuagint, but Matthew did, characteristically looking past Mark to Mark's biblical source; on checking Psalm 21 (Heb. 22) in the Septuagint, Matthew found in verse eight, more of what he took to be a prediction of events at the cross—what the passers-by said to Jesus—and inserted his version of it between verses 29 and 30 of Mark 15, which are otherwise repeated almost verbatim:

> The passers-by hurled abuse at him; they wagged their heads and cried, "You would pull the temple down, would you, and build it in three days? Come down from the cross and save yourself, if you are indeed the Son of God." So too the chief priests with the elders mocked him: "He saved others," they said, "but he cannot save himself. King of Israel, indeed! Let him come down now from the cross, and then we will believe him. Did he trust in God? Let God rescue [*hrusasthō*] him if he wants him [*thelei auton*]—for he said he was God's Son." Even the bandits who were crucified with him taunted him in the same way. (Matt. 27:39-44)

Matthew has inserted his version of Septuagint Psalm 21 (22):8 into Mark's narrative: "He hoped in the Lord; let him deliver him [*hrusasathō auton*], let him save him, because he wants him [*thelei auton*]."

Out of Mark's statement that those who were crucified with Jesus taunted him even as did the bystanders, Luke has created yet another fiction in order to make the theological point that salvation is available to whoever asks in faith:

> One of the criminals who hung there with him taunted him: "Are not you the Messiah? Save yourself, and us." But the other rebuked him: "Have you no fear of God? You are under the same sentence as he. For us it is plain justice; we are paying the price for our misdeeds; but this man has done nothing wrong." And he said, "Jesus, remember me when you come to your throne." He answered, "I tell you this: today you shall be with me in paradise." (Luke 23:39-43)

Mark (or his sources) wrote that, at the moment of Jesus' death, "the curtain of the temple was torn in two from top to bottom" (15:38), turning a first-century theological concept into an event. According to Exodus this curtain served as a "clear separation for you between the Holy Place and the Holy of Holies" (26:33)— a boundary marking off the holiest part of the temple, enterable only by the high priest. This notion was given special meaning by early Christians, for according to the Letter to the Hebrews,

> the priests are always entering the first tent in the discharge of their duties; but the second is entered only once a year, and by the high priest alone, and even then he must take with him the blood which he offers on his own behalf and for the people's sins of ignorance. . . . All this is symbolic, pointing to the present time. . . . But now Christ has come, high priest of good things already in being. . .; the blood of his sacrifice is his own blood. . .; and thus he has entered the sanctuary once and for all and secured an eternal deliverance. (Heb. 9:6–12)

Jesus, by his death, entered the Holy of Holies (i.e., the presence of God) to present his blood for our redemption. The consequence for the Christian is that "The blood of Jesus makes us free to enter boldly into the sanctuary by the new, living way which he has opened for us through the curtain of his flesh" (Heb. 10:19–20). This notion became, in Mark's Gospel, historicized: if Jesus opened the way for us into the sanctuary "through the curtain," then the curtain must have been opened, "torn in two from top to bottom."

VII

RESURRECTION FICTIONS

The earliest extended statement about the Easter experiences appears not in the Gospels but in Paul's first letter to the Corinthians. It dates from the early 50's, some twenty years after the crucifixion. Viewed in the light of the Gospel accounts of the resurrection, Paul's statement is as interesting for what it does not say as for what it does:

> I handed on to you the facts which had been imparted to me: that Christ died for our sins, in accordance with the Scriptures; that he was buried; that he was raised to life on the third day, according to the Scriptures; and that he appeared to Cephas, and afterwards to the Twelve. Then he appeared to over five hundred of our brothers at once, most of whom are still alive, though some have died. Then he appeared to James, and afterwards to all the apostles. (15:2-7)

None of these appearances, in anything like the sequence Paul lists, is depicted in the four Gospels. Moreover, not one of the Gospel resurrection appearances is identical with those listed by Paul. Paul did not know the Gospel resurrection stories, for the simple reason that they had not yet been invented, and the four evangelists, who wrote twenty to fifty years after Paul, either did not know his list of appearances or chose to ignore it. Perhaps most surprising of all the differences is Paul's failure to mention the legend of the empty tomb, which was, for the writer of the earliest Gospel (Mark), the only public, visible evidence for the resurrection. Though Paul vigorously attempts to convince the Christians at Corinth, some of whom apparently doubted, that Jesus indeed rose from the dead ("if Christ was not raised, your faith has nothing in it"—15:17), he never mentions this most striking piece of evidence. Indeed, he had probably never heard of it; it was a legend that grew up in Christian communities different from his own. It may even have post-dated his death, for Mark wrote almost twenty years after this letter to Corinth. Worse yet, Paul would not have agreed with Mark's theology even had he known it; for Paul, resurrection meant not the resuscitation of a corpse involving the removal of a stone and the emptying of a tomb, but a transformation from a dead physical body to a living spiritual one: "Flesh and blood can never possess the kingdom of God" (I Cor. 15:50).

Not only is Paul apparently unaware of the resurrection narratives recorded in the Gospels, but his own list of appearances is irreconcilable with those of the evangelists written later. Paul has it that the first appearance of the risen Lord was to Cephas (he always calls Peter by his Aramaic name, and apparently knows no stories about him in Greek). The Gospels describe no initial resurrection appearance to Peter (some women, the number varying from three to two to one, see him first), though Luke says that Peter did see him. According to the equally irreconcilable accounts in the Gospels, the first appearance was to Mary Magdala alone

(John), or to Mary Magdala and the other Mary (Matthew), or to Mary Magdala, Joanna, and Mary, the mother of James (Luke). Again, Paul declares that the second resurrection appearance was to the "twelve," whereas both Matthew and Luke stress that the appearance before the disciples was to the "eleven," Judas being dead. Either Paul did not know the story about the defection and suicide of Judas Iscariot or else the "twelve" meant something different to him.

In other words, different centers of early Christianity produced their own collections of evidence for Jesus' resurrection; these grew up independently and had, in the cases considered so far, almost nothing to do with each other. Of course, the most famous of the stories appear in the Gospels. Already in the mid-first century A.D., when Paul first wrote to the Corinthians, the idea was well established that Jesus rose again "on the third day, according to the Scriptures" (15:34). That is to say, Christians had scoured the Old Testament for passages that could, out of context, be interpreted as ancient oracles about the career of Jesus. This involved interpretive methods that to modern eyes seem bizarre. Matthew's assertion, in 21:4-5, based on his failure to understand the parallelism in the language of Zech. 9:9, that Jesus rode into Jerusalem astride two animals at once, is such an example. Moreover, the length of Jesus' stay in the tomb was computed by reading Hosea 6:1–2 out of context, it being the only passage in the Old Testament with an "on the third day" allusion:

> Come, let us return to the LORD;
> for he has torn us and will heal us,
>   he has struck us and he will bind up our wounds;
> after two days he will revive us,
> on the third day he will restore us,
>   that in his presence we may live.

Hosea is, in these verses, not discussing the career of a holy man seven hundred years in the future. He is addressing his own countrymen in his own time, calling upon a corrupt people for moral and religious reform, berating a people of whom one could say:

> Their deeds are outrageous.
> At Israel's sanctuary I have seen a horrible thing:
>   there Ephraim played the wanton
> and Israel defiled himself. (Hos. 6:10)

Some early Christians were aware of the paucity of Old Testament predictions about the length of Jesus' stay in the tomb, and set about to invent more. Matthew's additional evidence contains a prophecy in conflict with his own resurrection narrative. According to this evangelist, Jesus was buried on Friday just before sundown, and the tomb was found empty at sunrise on Sunday; thus, Jesus was presumably in the tomb two nights and one day. Nonetheless, Matthew imputed to Jesus the following, composed out of the Book of Jonah: "Jonah was in the sea-monster's belly for three days and three nights, and in the same way the Son of Man will be three days and three nights in the bowels of the earth" (Matt. 12:40).

The oldest Christian narrative describing the discovery of the empty tomb on the third day appears in the Gospel of Mark:

When the sabbath was over, Mary of Magdala, Mary the mother of James, and Salome bought aromatic oils intending to go and anoint him; and very early on the Sunday morning, just after sunrise, they came to the tomb. They were wondering among themselves who would roll away the stone for them from the entrance to the tomb, when they looked up and saw that the stone, huge as it was, had been rolled back already. They went into the tomb, where they saw a youth sitting on the right-hand side, wearing a white robe; and they were dumbfounded. But he said to them, "Fear nothing; you are looking for Jesus of Nazareth, who was crucified. He has been raised again; he is not here; look, there is the place where they laid him. But go and give this message to his disciples and Peter: 'He is going on before you into Galilee; there you will see him, as he told you.'" Then they went out and ran away from the tomb, beside themselves with terror. They said nothing to anybody, for they were afraid. (Mark 16:1-8)

The most ancient manuscripts of Mark end at this point, one of the strangest and most unsatisfying moments in all the Bible, depicting fear and silence on Easter morning and lacking a resurrection appearance. But within about fifty years, at least five separate attempts were made by various Christian imaginations to rewrite Mark's bare and disappointing story; they appear in the Long Ending and the Short Ending of Mark, and in the Gospels of Matthew, Luke, and John. The first two are second-century interpolations in some texts of Mark and are identified as such in any responsible modern text. They are Mark 16:9-20 (in the King James Version and others based on late manuscripts), an unskillful paraphrase of resurrection appearances in other Gospels; and Mark 16:9 in a few other late manuscripts, in which the women followed the youth's instructions to tell the disciples, a statement that conflicts with verse 8 of the original text.

Probably the first large-scale effort to rewrite Mark's account and make it more pleasing to the faithful took place when the Gospel of Matthew was written in the last two decades of the first century. Although the major written source of his information was the Gospel of Mark, Matthew made striking changes in Mark's resurrection narrative. Mark's account ends with the women running away from the tomb in terror and in their fear saying nothing to anybody. Matthew did not like this ending, however, so he changed it, consciously constructing a fictional narrative that more closely fit what he and his Christian community wanted to have happen on Easter morning: "They hurried away from the tomb in awe and great joy, and ran to tell the disciples" (Matt. 28:8). How did Matthew feel justified in making such a major change in Mark, a source he obviously regarded, for the most part, as authoritative? The answer is that Matthew was a conscious literary artist who sincerely believed in the resurrection; moreover, he believed he had the authority, granted him by his church and by its interpretation of the Old Testament, to "correct" Mark's Gospel and theology. Indeed, he had already corrected Mark many times before, often doing so on the basis of what he regarded as his superior understanding of the oracles in the Old Testament. For since Jesus' life happened "according to the Scriptures," early Christians were confident that in order to find out about him, they did not need to engage in historical research or consult witnesses (in our understanding of these two approaches); they found detailed history in the ancient oracles of the Hebrew Bible, read as a book about Jesus.

Matthew was a careful student both of the Old Testament and of Mark, which in his time was not yet accepted as canonical Scripture and thus could be changed at need. His study revealed how frequently Mark's Gospel was transparent upon Scripture (or based upon it), and in ways that Mark himself apparently did not recognize. Mark had composed his Gospel on the basis of earlier oral and written sources, which in turn had found much of their information about Jesus in the Old Testament. Though Mark seems not to have realized that this was so, Matthew readily recognized the relationships between Mark and the Old Testament, and even took it upon himself to extend and correct them. In this case he saw Mark's resurrection narrative as transparent upon the Book of Daniel, especially chapter 6, the story of the lion's den. On recognizing the relationship, Matthew seems to have consulted the Septuagint version of Daniel and believed that he found there details of a more accurate account of the happenings of that Sunday morning some sixty years before, than could be found in the pages of Mark; never mind that Daniel's narrative is a story in the past tense about presumed events in the distant past. Matthew ignored its narrative and historical content and turned it into a prophetic oracle, as had the originators of Mark's story.

It seems clear that in a literary sense at least, Matthew was right: the account of the empty tomb used by Mark was indeed structured on Daniel's story of the lion's den. In the 30's and 40's, the empty tomb story was not part of the tradition about the resurrection; Paul was quite unaware of it. The legend grew in Mark's community, or one from which it borrowed, as part of its stock of evidence for Jesus' resurrection. As Matthew was to do again nearly a generation later, certain Christians, perhaps in the 50's or 60's, searched the Old Testament, a major source of what was for them authoritative information about Jesus, in order to construct their account of the passion and resurrection, and found in the Book of Daniel much of what they needed. Consider the parallels: a leader of the nation opposed to the spokesman for God's people (Darius of Persia; Joseph of Arimathea), yet one who in his heart reveres that spokesman (Daniel; Jesus), though greatly distressed, feels obliged to place the spokesman into a pit in the ground and cover it with a stone (the lion's den; the tomb), an act that clearly means the spokesman's permanent end. In both stories the death of the spokesman is required by law (the law of the Medes and Persians; the law of Rome), and in both, the executor of that law is reluctant to enforce it (Darius "exerted himself until evening" to save Daniel; Pilate attempted to convince an angry mob that Jesus should be released). But despite reluctance and delay, late in the afternoon both heroes are placed into the pit. In both stories a stone is put over the opening, and in both the placer of the stone has hope in the providence of God (Darius says, "Your own God . . . will save you"; Joseph "looked forward to the kingdom of God"). Early on a subsequent morning in both stories ("At dawn, as soon as it was light"—Dan. 6:19, "just after sunrise"—Mark 16:2), the pit is approached by those who cared deeply for the hero (Darius; the three women). Next comes joyful news (Daniel lives; "He has been raised again"). In both stories, the stone is removed, death is miraculously overcome, and deliverance is assisted by an angel ("My God sent his angel," to shut the lions' mouths, says Daniel; "a young man . . . dressed in a white robe" has removed the stone, says Mark).

As Matthew studied Mark's account, he perceived its transparence upon Daniel, and found in the latter not only the literary source of the empty tomb story (which because of that particular first-century orientation he recognized as a prophecy rather than as a source), but also the means of both enlarging and clarifying Mark and of overcoming what he regarded as its deficiencies. The modern reader who grasps the dependence of Mark on Daniel might be led to see the gospel narrative as a carefully constructed fiction which in the absence of real evidence is based on a belief in what must have been the case, since Daniel had "predicted" it. Matthew's reaction was in keeping with first-century oracular views of the Old Testament: any detail in Mark which differs from Matthew's interpretation of Daniel's "prediction" must be historically inaccurate. For example, Mark does not make it clear enough to Matthew's satisfaction that the figure the women see at the tomb is an angel (*aggelos*) as Daniel had clearly called him; Mark's figure is merely a youth (*neaniskon*) in a white robe. For the sake of prophetic fulfilment, Matthew changed "youth" to "angel of the Lord" (Matt. 28:2). Moreover, since Mark does not describe the figure in terms unmistakably angelic, Matthew alters the description, again on the basis of the Septuagint version of Daniel, where he finds a heavenly being whose "raiment was white as snow" (*to enduma autou leukon hosei chion*—Dan. 7:9); thus Matthew's angel has "raiment white as snow" (*to enduma auto leukon hōs chion*—Matt. 28:3). Matthew's angel has a spectacular mien: "His appearance was like lightning" (*ēn de hē eidea autou hōs astrapē*—Matt. 28:3), as in Daniel, who says of an angel that "his face was as the appearance of lightning" (*to prosōpon autou hōs hē horasis astrapēs*—Dan. 10:6). Mark's figure says, "Do not be amazed" (*Mē ekthambeisthe*—16:5); Matthew, however, knowing that angels, when they appear, say, "Do not be afraid" (*Mē phobou*—Dan. 10:12), changes the opening of the angel's speech to the women to accord with the Old Testament: "Do not be afraid" (*Mē phobeisthe*—Matt. 28:5). Finally, Matthew found in Daniel justification for changing Mark's statement that the announcement of the resurrection left the women only fearful and silent: When Darius learned that Daniel was still alive, "the king was very glad" (6:23). Thus Matthew declares that the women, on learning that "he is risen," reacted with "awe and great joy" (Matt. 28:8).

Matthew was equally unhappy with yet another aspect of Mark's account, and invented more fiction to replace it. In Mark, the women "bought aromatic oils intending to go and anoint" Jesus' body on the Sunday after his death. As they approached the sepulchre, they "were wondering among themselves who would roll away the stone for them from the entrance to the tomb, when they looked up and saw that the stone, huge as it was, had been rolled back already" (Mark 16:1-4). The dissatisfied Matthew radically changes the account, saying that it was

> about daybreak on Sunday, when Mary of Magdala and the other Mary came to look at the grave. Suddenly there was a violent earthquake; an angel of the Lord descended from heaven; he came to the stone and rolled it away. (Matt. 28:1-2)

In part, Matthew made the change because he disagreed with Mark's resurrection theology. Mark apparently believed that the resurrected Jesus was a resuscitated corpse, who required that the stone be moved for him before he could leave the tomb, but Matthew's view was closer to Paul's—the resurrected Jesus had a spiritual body. Thus Matthew writes that the women came not to find that the stone had been rolled back already, but as they watched, the angel removed the stone from an already empty tomb, Jesus earlier having passed through the stone.

But Matthew had an even more urgent task than correcting theology; he had to deal with a pressing apologetic problem: unbelievers living in his district (thought to be Antioch) were scoffing that Jesus had not been resurrected, that his disciples had merely stolen the body and circulated a lie. In fact, says Matthew, this claim "is current in Jewish circles to this day" (28:25). What for Mark had been the only visible evidence *for* the resurrection had become powerful evidence *against* the resurrection. Matthew's solution to this apologetic problem is a brilliant fiction. Note how subtly he changes the women's intention: in Mark they had gone "intending to anoint his body"; in Matthew they "came to look at the grave." Matthew also deletes a whole sentence from his Markan source: "They were wondering among themselves who would roll away the stone for them" (Mark 16:3). He does so because it is inconsistent with the text of his composition found at the end of chapter 27:

> Next day, the morning after that Friday, the chief priests and the Pharisees came in a body to Pilate. "Your Excellency," they said, "we recall how that imposter said while he was still alive, 'I am to be raised again after three days.' So will you give orders for the grave to be made secure until the third day? Otherwise his disciples may come, steal the body and then tell the people that he has been raised from the dead; and the final deception will be worse than the first." "You may have your guard," said Pilate; "go and make it secure as best you can." So they went and made the grave secure; they sealed the stone, and left the guard in charge. (Matt. 27:62-66)

The women in Matthew could not be allowed the intention of anointing Jesus' body, for in his fiction guards were posted at the tomb precisely to keep anyone from touching the remains (no guards, of course, are mentioned in the other Gospels).

Once again, Matthew has constructed a conscious literary fiction based on what he convinced himself was a prophecy more accurate than Mark's history—one again found in the Book of Daniel. There in 6:17 LXX the prophet declares that when Daniel was placed in the lions' den, a "stone [*lithon*] was brought and put over the mouth of the pit, and the king sealed [*esphragisato*] it." Ample biblical justification existed for Matt. 27:66 to impute to Pilate orders that his men should secure the tomb by "sealing the stone" (*sphragisantes ton lithon*).

Having put the guards there, Matthew must also find a way to get rid of them; he found it in the same chapter of Daniel that provided his description of the angel. When Daniel saw an angel whose "face shone like lightning," he found himself "trembling": "I fell prone on the ground in a trance" (Dan. 10:6,9). Thus, when the angel of the Lord, whose "face shone like lightning," appeared at Jesus' tomb, "the guards shook with fear and lay like the dead" (Matt. 28:3-4). In this way, Matthew outflanks a serious apologetic problem raised by the abruptness of Mark's ending: the empty tomb had become an embarrassment to be overcome, and Matthew's fiction of the guard and the removal of the stone from the already empty tomb neatly solves the problem. If Matthew could next supply the resurrection appearances Mark lacks, the empty tomb would no longer be needed as evidence that "he has been raised again"; for in Matthew the stone did not need to be removed to show that Jesus lived—invisible, he had already passed through it and was now about to appear to the women.

Matthew depicts two appearances of the risen Jesus, one to the women at the tomb and one to the disciples in Galilee. The first is little more than a recapitulation of the angelic youth's speech in Mark supplemented by yet another reference to Psalm 22; the second is a pastiche of passages from Daniel. Remember that in Mark the youth in a white robe says to the women,

"He has been raised again; he is not here; look, there is the place where they laid him. But go and give this message to his disciples and Peter: 'He is going on before you into Galilee; there you will see him, as he told you.'" (Mark 16:6-7)

For his own dramatic purposes, Matthew changes the end of the youth's speech; he does not wish to spoil the effect of Jesus' speech inserted two verses later; in Matthew the angel says to the women:

> "Go quickly and tell his disciples, 'He has been raised from the dead and is going on before you into Galilee; there you will see him.' That is what I had to tell you." (Matt 28:7)

The women then run out in great joy to obey the angel, when "suddenly Jesus was there in their path." They react suitably, as does Daniel when he sees the angel Gabriel: "I fell with my face to the earth" (Dan. 10:9); thus, at the sight of Jesus, the women fell "prostrate before him" (Matt. 28:9). Just as suitably, Jesus' first words to the women are the same as those of the angel to Daniel: "Do not be afraid" (Dan. 10:9; Matt. 28:10). The rest of Jesus' speech, with one change out of the Old Testament, is essentially a restatement of what the youth in Mark had already said: "Go and take word to my brothers that they are to leave for Galilee. They will see me there" (Matt. 28:10). Matthew changed the words spoken by the youth in Mark's gospel from, "There you will see him, as he told you" to "There you will see him. That is what I had to tell you"; because Jesus in Matthew's account will say a few moments later, "They will see me there," Matthew could not allow the angel to say "as he told you," for Jesus has not yet said it. Note also that Matthew's Jesus says, "Take word to my brothers," whereas the angel has said, "Tell his disciples." Here Matthew has returned to Psalm 22 as the source of Jesus' words: "I will declare thy name to my brothers" (*tois adelphois mou*—Ps. 21 [22]:22 LXX); hence Matthew's *apaggeilate tois adelphois mou.*

Jesus' appearance to the disciples in Galilee at chapter 28, verse 16: "The eleven disciples made their way to Galilee, to the mountain where Jesus had told them to meet him," is again a pastiche of passages in Daniel, introduced by a fascinating lapse on Matthew's part; for Jesus has done no such thing, either in

Matthew or Mark. Matthew has invented and assumed the prior saying. When the disciples see Jesus in Galilee, they react as did Daniel, whose book is the source of this second appearance: "They fell prostrate before him."

For Jesus' speech two verses later—

"Full authority in heaven and on earth has been committed to me. Go therefore and make all nations my disciples; baptize men everywhere in the name of the Father and the Son and the Holy Spirit, and teach them to observe all that I have commanded you. And be assured, I am with you always, to the end of time."

—Matthew has combined different Greek versions of Daniel:

Edothe moi pasa exousia	*autō edothē hē archē . . . hē exousia auto*
Given to me all authority	to him given the rule . . . the authority of him
	(Dan. 7:14 LXX)

exousia en ouranō kai epi tēs gēs	*exousian echein panton tōn en to ouranō*
authority in heaven and upon	authority to hold all in the heaven
earth	*kai epi tēs ges*
	and upon the earth
	(Dan. 7:14 Theodotion)

Jesus' command to "make all nations my disciples" is Matthew's rendering of Daniel's "All nations, tribes, and languages shall serve him." Since Matthew regarded the risen Jesus as the soon-to-return Son of Man, it seemed appropriate to him to construct this speech on Daniel's description there of the coming of the Son of Man to assume the everlasting kingdom. The trinitarian baptismal formula in the next part of Jesus' speech seems an interpolation into the text of Matthew. According to Acts 2:38, the first-century baptismal formula was "in the name of Jesus the Messiah"; even in the late third century Eusebius, quoting Matthew 28:19, wrote, "Make disciples of all nations in my name." The trinitarian formula represents a theology later than Matthew's and shows the freedom with which early Christians approached the text of the New Testament—treating Matthew as freely as Matthew treated Mark.

The last verse of Matthew (28:20), "I am with you always, to the end of time [*ego meth' humon eimi pasas tas hemeras heos tes sunteleias tou aionos*]"—to me the most beautiful and moving statement in all of Scripture—shows the evangelist's great literary skill. It represents a combination of earlier sayings by Jesus and Daniel's final prediction in that book's last verse: "The harvest is the end of the age [*sunteleia aionos*]" (Matt. 13:39); "Where two or three are met together in my name, I am there with them" (Matt. 18:20); "end of the days [*sunteleian hemeron*]" (Dan. 12:13).

In sum, we may say that Matthew's account of the resurrection is a fictional enlargement of Mark's fictional narrative, produced, at least in part, because of what he saw as the incomplete and inadequate nature of Mark's last chapter. Certainly, Matthew sincerely believed in the resurrection; he also believed that his version of the story was more authoritative, more "scriptural," than Mark's, but his sincerity does not make his story less fictive. The same may be said of Luke's enlargement of the Markan resurrection account.

The Gospel of Luke is, like that of Matthew, an expanded revision of Mark. Of Mark's 661 verses, some 360 appear in Luke, either word-for-word or with deliberate changes. Some of the most dramatic of these changes appear in Luke's version of Mark's resurrection narrative. Here once again is part of Mark's account:

> "He has been raised again; he is not here; look, there is the place where they laid him. But go and give this message to his disciples and Peter: 'He is going on before you into Galilee; there you will see him, as he told you.'" Then they went out and ran away from the tomb, beside themselves with terror. They said nothing to anybody, for they were afraid. (Mark 16:6-8)

Luke's is strikingly different:

> Finding that the stone had been rolled away from the tomb, they went inside; but the body was not to be found. While they stood utterly at a loss, all of a sudden two men in dazzling garments were at their side. They were terrified, and stood with eyes cast down, but the men said, "Why search among the dead for one who lives? Remember what he told you while he was still in Galilee, about the Son of Man: how he must be given up into the power of sinful men and be crucified, and must rise again on the third day." Then they recalled his words and, returning from the tomb, they reported all this to the Eleven and all the others. (Luke 24:2-9)

What prompted Luke to make such radical changes in Mark, a source he relied on heavily, having already used more than three hundred of its verses? In part, the answer is exactly parallel to the case in Matthew. Quite independently of Matthew, Luke also perceived that Mark was transparent upon the Book of Daniel, and went directly to the latter for some of his variations from Mark. But he found details different from those used by Matthew. Whereas Matthew had taken Daniel's attribution to the angel at the tomb a face that shone like lightning, Luke applied this detail to the angel's clothing, for the "dazzling garments" in Luke are literally "lightning-like" (*astraptouse*—Luke 24:4). Luke borrows another detail from the same chapter of Daniel, or perhaps from a type-scene in the Old Testament. When Daniel sees the angel, he says, "I turned my face to the ground" (*edoka to prosopon mou epi ten gen*—Dan. 10:15 LXX); thus in Luke, at the sight of the angels, the women "turned their faces to the ground" (*klinouson ta prosopa eis ten gen*—Luke 24:5). There is a parallel between this and the Septuagint Genesis account as source of yet another telling change Luke works upon Mark—the shift from one youth to "two men." Like Matthew, Luke was steeped in the language of the Septuagint, and it was perhaps this familiarity that lies behind the change. In Genesis, when Lot sees "two angels" (*duo aggeloi*), "he worshipped with his face to the ground" (*prosekunēse tō pro-sōpō epi tēn gēn*—Gen. 19:1 LXX). Conjoining these verses allowed, or caused, Luke to change a single youth in a white robe to two men in dazzling garments. Perhaps the reason Luke calls them "men" (*andres*) rather than angels is that the "two angels" of Gen. 19:1 are described in verse two of the preceding chapter as "men," (*andres*).

Luke's most significant change from Mark—the totally different angelic message at the tomb—finds its origin not in the Old Testament, however, but in Luke's need to prepare his readers for the story of Pentecost in the Book of Acts, which he also wrote. In the version of the story Luke wishes to present, the disciples cannot be ordered, or even allowed, to leave Jerusalem for Galilee; they must remain for the all-important Pentecost experience. Thus the angels say to the women not, "He is going on before you into Galilee; there you will see him," but, "Remember what he told you while he was still in Galilee, about the Son of Man: how he must be given up into the power of sinful men and be crucified, and must rise again on the third day." Mark says that there will be a resurrection appearance in Galilee, but ends before describing it, at least in the copies possessed by Matthew and Luke.

Matthew composed a Galilee resurrection appearance using the Book of Daniel as the source of what Jesus would have said. But Luke eliminates the angel's statement that the risen Jesus is going to Galilee; in contrast to Matthew, who composes a new statement for Jesus out of the youth's speech in Mark ("Take word to my brothers that they are to leave for Galilee"—Matt. 28:10), Luke imputes to Jesus a new saying that demands quite the opposite: "Stay here in this city until you are armed with the power from above" (Luke 24:49). Luke thus presents resurrection appearances only in the vicinity of Jerusalem. Mark implies, and Matthew specifically declares, that Jesus, followed later by his disciples, left Jerusalem immediately after his resurrection and went to Galilee, some eighty or ninety miles to the north, where they all met. Luke writes in (Acts 1:3-4) that the risen Jesus "over a period of forty days . . . appeared to them and taught them about the kingdom of God. While he was in their company he told them not to leave Jerusalem." For Luke, the story of Pentecost, described in the second chapter of Acts, overshadowed any assertion that the disciples were in Galilee meeting Jesus; they had to be in Jerusalem, so he placed them there and constructed a saying by Jesus to justify this change.

The fourth evangelist, John (who was not the Apostle, but a Christian who wrote at the very end of the first century), possessed a collection of resurrection narratives different from those used by Matthew and Luke, and irreconcilable with them. In Luke, when the women returned to the disciples with the joyous news that the tomb was empty and that two angels had declared Jesus risen, "The story appeared to them to be nonsense, and they would not believe" (24:11); but in John, when Peter and the other disciples hear the women's message, they run to the tomb and find it empty, whereat, says John, they "believed" (20:28). Hence, in Luke it is the women who believe, and the disciples who doubt, while in John it is the disciples who believe, while Mary Magdalene doubts, still assuming that someone has removed Jesus' corpse: "They have taken my Lord away, and I do not know where they have laid him" (20:13). Then, in John as in Matthew, the risen Jesus appears, but in the former he appears to Mary Magdalene alone; in the latter, two women, both named Mary, witness him. Moreover, when the women see Jesus, they "clasped his feet, falling prostrate before him" (28:9), while Mary Magdalene fails to recognize him, "Thinking it was the gardener" (John 20:15); when she finally comprehends his identity, he refuses to allow her to touch him. Matthew and Mark write that Jesus is leaving for Galilee where his disciples must follow and meet him; Luke writes that they must *not* leave Jerusalem; while John insists that Jesus is neither leaving for Galilee nor staying in Jerusalem; he is going straight to heaven: "I am now ascending to my Father" (20:17). John has drawn on a different source for what the risen Jesus says, the Septuagint

Book of Tobit, and for reasons similar to Matthew's and Luke's use of Daniel. John sees through his sources (Mark and Luke, or sources common to the three) to Tobit, reading it as a prophetic picture of Easter morning and providing a striking example of what can be called a literary convention about the appearance and speech of a heavenly figure.

The Book of Tobit is a work of religious fiction, written perhaps in the second century B.C., which presents a widespread Mediterranean-world soteriological myth: the descent of a heavenly figure as a man who performs saving acts, reveals his true identity, and returns to heaven. As we might expect, he declares his identity with the ancient-world formula of divine self-revelation: "I am" (cf. Ex. 6:3 and John 8:58), a statement that has the conventional effect. When the angel says, "I am Raphael" (*Egō eimi Hraphaēl* —Tob. 12:15 LXX), Tobit and his son "fell upon their faces" (*epeson epi prosōpon*—12:16), just as when Jesus reveals himself to Judas and the soldiers, saying, "I am" (*Egō eimi*), they "fell to the ground" (*epesan chamai*—John 18:5, 6).

John appears to know from Luke that when the risen Jesus appears to his disciples in Jerusalem, he says, "Peace be with you" (*eirēnē humin*—Luke 24:36 in mss. Sinaiticus, Alexandrinus, and Vaticanus); however, John may have possessed a copy of Luke in which Jesus speaks in the formula of Raphael in Tobit: "Peace be with you. . . . do not be afraid" (It., Vg., Sy^p), or "Do not be afraid; peace be with you" (W). Luke and Matthew found "Do not be afraid" in Daniel; I argue that John saw through Luke (or a parallel) to Tobit, in which Raphael says at the time of his self-revelation, "Do not be afraid; peace be with you" (*mē phobeisthe, eirēnē humin*—Tob. 12:16 LXX); thus, John 20:19: "Peace be with you" (*Eirēnē humin*).

According to John, the first resurrection appearance was to Mary Magdalene, to whom Jesus says words found in no other Gospel: "I am ascending to my father" (*Anabainō pros ton patera mou*—John 20:17), but which echo Tobit's declaration: "I am ascending to him who sent me" (*anabainō pros ton aposteilanta me*—12:20 LXX). The one "who sent me" is, of course, "our Lord, God our Father" (Tob. 13:4), just as Jesus is "ascending to my Father and your Father, my God and your God" (John 20:17). When Mary first saw Jesus, she "did not know" (*ouk ēdei*—John 20:14) that it was he, just as when Tobias first saw Raphael, he "did not know" (*ouk ēdei*—Tob. 5:5) he was an angel.

John's second resurrection appearance, on the evening of the same day, follows the literary conventions established by Daniel and Tobit: "Late that Sunday evening . . . Jesus came and stood among them. 'Peace be with you!' he said" (*Eirēnē humin*—John 20:19). The same convention appears in their response: "When the disciples saw the Lord, they were filled with joy" (John 20:20). When Darius learned that Daniel was alive he "was overjoyed" (Dan. 6:23); when Tobit and his son learned that their helper was in fact the angel Raphael, they were at first "fearful, and fell upon their faces," but on being reassured, Tobit composed a "prayer of rejoicing" (Tob. 12:16; 13:1).

Like Luke, John possessed a legend that the Holy Spirit came upon the disciples not long after the resurrection, but John's story is altogether different from Luke's account of Pentecost (the descent of the Spirit fifty days after the Passion—Acts 2). Whereas Luke's version delays the gift of the Holy Spirit some seven weeks, John's shows it happening on the first Easter Sunday, during the second resurrection appearance: "Then he breathed on them, saying, 'Receive the Holy Spirit'" (John 20:22). John's third resurrection-appearance story is the beautiful and touching account of doubting Thomas, who responds with Tobit's words upon learning that his helper is Raphael: "our Lord, and God our Father" (*Kurios hēmōn, kai Theos autos patēr hēmōn*—Tob. 13:4); Thomas responds, "My Lord and my God!" (*Ho kurios mou kai ho theos mou*—John 20:28). This story reveals its apologetic purpose in Jesus' last words to Thomas: "Because you have seen me you have found faith. Happy are they who never saw me and yet have found faith"

(John 20:29). It is a pity that this powerful story ("Reach your hand here and put it into my side") had not yet been invented when Paul first wrote to the disbelieving Corinthians.

The Gospel of John, as originally written (circa 100 A.D.), ended immediately after Jesus' appearance before the doubting Thomas, with this obviously concluding summary:

> There were indeed many other signs that Jesus performed in the presence of his disciples, which are not recorded in this book. Those here written have been recorded in order that you may hold the faith that Jesus is the Christ, the Son of God, and that through this faith you may possess life by his name. (20:30-31)

Early in the second century, however, certain Christians to whom the gospels of Matthew and Luke were important, recognized that both these earlier works stress, in opposition to John, that the resurrection appearances occurred in Galilee as well as Jerusalem. They took it upon themselves to reconcile John with the others by adding a twenty-first chapter. That this section is not by the author of the rest of the Gospel is clear from the prominence it gives to the "sons of Zebedee" (John 21:2), who are mentioned by this name nowhere else in the Fourth Gospel, though they are central figures in the Synoptics. A major purpose of the addition, and another sign of its late date, is betrayed by the last saying attributed to Jesus in the chapter. For no reason apparent in the narrative, we are told that Peter "saw" an unnamed disciple, the one "whom Jesus loved," and asked Jesus, "What will happen to him?" Jesus' response was, "If it should be my will that he wait until I come, what is that to you? Follow me."

> That saying of Jesus became current in the brotherhood, and was taken to mean that the disciple would not die. But in fact Jesus did not say that he would not die; he only said "If it should be my will that he should wait until I come, what is that to you?" (21:21-23)

Obviously this disciple (in fact *all* the first-generation Christians) *had* long since died, and Jesus showed no signs of returning; the tradition persisted, however, that those were the words of Jesus, for the first generation indeed confidently expected the early return of their Lord (had he not said, in Mark 9:1, "There are some of those standing here who will not taste death before they have seen the kingdom of God already come"?) A saying had to be constructed that would not only demystify and reinterpret this persistent legend, so troubling to the faithful, but solve the apologetic problem it presented. Chapter 21 exists, in part, for this purpose; and though the attempt is an unconvincing quibble, it had to be made.

The resurrection narratives in the last chapters of the four Gospels are effective stories that have given solace and hope to millions of believers who have not read them carefully. Anyone who does read them carefully finds multiple reasons to change them. This is what happened when each Gospel writer read an earlier narrative.

NOTES

I

1. See *The Life and Times of Apollonius of Tyana*, trans. Charles P. Eells (New York: AMS, 1967).

2. Mircea Eliade, *Cosmos and History: The Myth of the Eternal Return* (New York: Harper and Row, 1959), p. 39.

3. See Hayden White, *Metahistory* (Baltimore: Johns Hopkins, 1973) and *Tropics of Discourse* (Baltimore: Johns Hopkins, 1978).

4. B. H. Streeter, *The Four Gospels: A Study of Origins* (London: Macmillan, 1951), p. 383.

5. Reginald H. Fuller, *The Formation of the Resurrection Narratives* (New York: Macmillan, 1971), p. 63.

6. Norman Perrin, *What Is Redaction Criticism?* (Philadelphia: Fortress, 1969), p. 17.

7. I shall hold to the by-now standard notion that Mark was written about 70 A.D., Matthew and Luke in the 80's or 90's, and John about 100 A.D. John A. T. Robinson's effort, *Redating the New Testament*, to place all the writing before 70 A.D., does not convince me.

8. Northrop Frye, *The Great Code: The Bible and Literature* (New York: Harcourt Brace, 1982), p. 78.

II

1. Streeter, *The Four Gospels*, p. 164.

2. *Documents for the Study of the Gospels*, ed. David R. Cartlidge and David L. Dungan (Cleveland: Collins, 1980), pp. 13–14.

3. *Ibid.*, p. 18.

4. *Ibid.*

5. *Ibid.*

6. Norman Perrin, *The New Testament: An Introduction* (New York: Harcourt, 1974), p. 279.

7. As quoted from the Gospel according to the Hebrews by Jerome in his *Commentary on Isaiah 11:2*; quoted in Burton H. Throckmorton, Jr., *Gospel Parallels: A Synopsis of the First Three Gospels* (Nashville: Thomas Nelson, 1979), p. 11.

8. Epiphanius, *Against Heresies* XXX.13.7–8, quoted in Throckmorton, p. 11.

9. *Jesus in History and Myth*, ed. R. Joseph Hoffmann and Gerald A. Larue (Buffalo: Prometheus, 1986), p. 143.

10. *Ibid.*, p. 150.

III

1. F. C. Conybeare, *The Origins of Christianity* (Evanston, Ill.: University Books, 1958), p. 206.

2. *Ibid.*, p. 188.

3. Plutarch, *Convivial Disputations*, viii, 1, 2, quoted in Conybeare, p. 188.

4. Conybeare, p. 180.

5. Diogenes Laertius, *Lives and Opinions of the Eminent Philosophers*, quoted in Conybeare, p. 195.

6. *Testament of Levi*, 18:3.

7. Cicero, *De Divinatione*, I:23, 47, quoted in the *Encyclopedia Biblica*, III, 3351.

8. Pliny, *Natural History*, 30, 16, cited in the *Encyclopedia Biblica*, III, 3351.

9. Dio Cassius, *Roman History*, 63, 2, trans. Earnest Carey (London: Heinemann, 1914).

10. Suetonius, *The Deified Augustus*, 94, trans. J. C. Rolfe (London: Heinemann, 1914).

11. *Ibid.*

12. *Jewish Encyclopedia* (New York: Ktav, N.D.), I, 86.

13. Raymond E. Brown, *The Birth of the Messiah* (New York: Doubleday, 1977), p. 413.

IV

1. Ernest Käsemann, *Essays on New Testament Themes*, trans. W. J. Montague (London: SCM Press, 1964), pp. 48, 50–51.

2. Rudolf Bultmann, *The Gospel of John* (Philadelphia: Westminster, 1971), p. 240.

3. *Ibid.*

4. *Ibid.*, p. 230.

V

1. Rudolf Bultmann, *John,* p. 238.

2. C. K. Barrett, *The Gospel According to St. John: An Introduction* (Philadelphia: Westminster, 1978), p. 249.

3. See Bultmann, *op. cit.*, and Robert Fortna, *The Gospel of Signs: A Reconstruction of the Narrative Source Underlying the Fourth Gospel* (Cambridge: At the University Press, 1965).

4. Robert Alter, *The Art of Biblical Narrative* (New York: Basic Books, 1981), p. 48.

5. Barrett, p. 356.

6. *Ibid.*, p. 352.

7. Morton Smith, *The Secret Gospel of Mark* (New York: Columbia, 1973), p. 92.

8. *Ibid.*, pp. 95, 61.

9. E. A. Wallis Budge, *The Book of the Dead: The Papyrus of Ani* (New York: Dover, 1967), p. ix.

10. *Ibid.*, p. xlix.

11. I accept the view of Streeter, Norman Perrin, and others that the author of the Fourth Gospel probably knew the Gospels of Mark and Luke.

12. R. O. Faulkner, *The Ancient Egyptian Pyramid Texts* (Oxford: Clarendon, 1969), p. 164.

13. E. A. Wallis Budge, *The Book of the Opening of the Mouth* (New York: Blom, 1972), p. 124.

14. *Ibid.*
15. Budge, *The Book of the Dead*, p. cxxxiv.
16. Faulkner, Utterance 670.
17. Streeter, *The Four Gospels*, p. 338.

VI

1. Vernon K. Robbins, "Last Meal: Preparation, Betrayal, and Absence (Mark 14:12–25)," in *The Passion in Mark*, ed. Werner H. Kelber (Philadelphia: Fortress, 1976), p. 23.
2. *Ibid.*, p. 25.
3. B. W. Bacon, "What Did Judas Betray?" *Hibbert Journal*, XIX (1920–21), 478.
4. Northrop Frye, *The Great Code*, p. 40.